THE STRAND THEATRE FIRE

The 1941 Brockton Tragedy and the Fallen Thirteen

JAMES E. BENSON & NICOLE B. CASPER

Foreword by Kenneth F. Galligan, Brockton Fire Chief, Retired

THE History PRESS

Published by The History Press
Charleston, SC
www.historypress.net

First published 2017

Manufactured in the United States

ISBN 9781467135276

Library of Congress Control Number: 2016956922

Notice: The information in this book is true and complete to the best of our knowledge. It is offered without guarantee on the part of the authors or The History Press. The authors and The History Press disclaim all liability in connection with the use of this book.

This book is dedicated to the thirteen firemen who responded to the Strand Theatre fire but never returned home.

Contents

Foreword

March 10, 1941, will forever be remembered in the history of the Brockton Fire Department as the date when thirteen courageous and dedicated firefighters lost their lives in the performance of duty at the Strand Theatre fire and building collapse.

Annually, nearly one hundred firefighters in the United States succumb to injuries sustained while responding to or operating at emergency scenes. Among the many dangers firefighters face while operating at a building fire is the sudden and unexpected collapse of the structure. Unfortunately, the history of the American Fire Service contains numerous instances where multiple firefighter deaths are attributed to failures in building design or construction. Over time, methods of building construction and materials change after lessons are learned following tragedies such as the Strand Theatre fire. Firefighting strategy and tactics are often revised and refined as widespread knowledge of firefighting tragedies become common knowledge by those charged with making fireground firefighting decisions.

One hallmark of firefighting that defines the character of a fire department is its ability to stop the spread of fire where it finds it. Every emergency scene presents a learning experience in concert with tried and proven past experiences. In most cases, this philosophy requires an aggressive interior attack of the fire that without a doubt requires competent leadership and a strong sense of commitment, courage, fortitude, skill and teamwork.

Foreword

This book stands as a tribute to the thirteen firefighters who lost their lives at the Strand Theatre fire and the Brockton Fire Department, a well-honed and experienced fire department whose members performed their duty protecting the lives and property in the city of Brockton.

Kenneth F. Galligan
Brockton Fire Chief, Retired

Acknowledgements

The success of a project like this is the result of support and assistance from a variety of people and institutions. This book would not have been possible without the support of members of the Brockton Fire Department, including Chief Michael F. Williams, Deputy Chief Kevin Galligan, Captain Edward Williams, fire alarm operator Bob Myers and Brockton Fire Fighters Local 144 president Archibald Gormley Jr. The Brockton Historical Society, Brockton Fire Museum and Brockton Public Library provided a wealth of resources in the research of this book, and for that, we are appreciative. In addition, we would like to acknowledge the late William A. Donovan, a retired Brockton firefighter and curator of the Brockton Fire Museum who was responsible for collecting and preserving many of the sources used in this book.

We would like to thank the following individuals who assisted us in obtaining or providing accounts of the fire and other valuable information, including Michael Zarella, Michael Sites, William Lipper, Eileen Kelley, Frederick Kelley, Alice LaLiberte Bruce, Nancy Many, Sara Carroll, Patricia Symes, Christine Newman, John Duggan, Chris Welch and Mary Welch.

A special expression of gratitude is given to the Stonehill College Archives, home of the Stanley A. Bauman Collection, and to students Amanda Berthold '16, Raymond Addison '16 and Angela Farias '18 for their countless hours scanning and editing hundreds of photos from the Bauman Collection for possible inclusion in this book under the direction of Jonathan Green, assistant archivist and digital assets manager. A huge debt of gratitude is also owed Jonathan Green for his support and countless hours of proofing and editing this manuscript. A word of thanks is also due to Cheryl McGrath, director of the Stonehill College Libraries, for her enthusiasm and unwavering support of this project.

A special thank-you goes to Amanda Irle, Julia Turner and the staff of The History Press for making this book possible. Their professionalism is above reproach and greatly appreciated.

We are most indebted to retired Brockton Fire Chief Kenneth F. Galligan, curator of the Brockton Fire Museum, not only for his graciousness in writing the foreword to this work but also for his decades-long commitment to preserving the history of the Brockton Fire Department and Strand Theatre fire. This book would not have been possible without his knowledge, support and technical advice.

Lastly, no book such as this would have been possible without the support of our families and friends. Nicole would like to thank her husband, Michael J. Casper; parents, Dean and Diane Tourangeau; and in-laws, James and Marianne Casper, for their excitement, patience and support during the writing of this book. She would also like to thank her family and friends for their ongoing support and encouragement. James would like to thank his family and friends for their continued support during the time that this book was in the process of being researched and written. He would also like to express his deep appreciation for the honor of having known some of the children of the victims of the fire as well as several of those firefighters who survived the blaze.

Introduction

Throughout the course of human history, it is not the good things that are most remembered. The tragic, the shocking, the heart-wrenching moments of life linger. Some fade while others live as though it was yesterday that they occurred. One such moment transpired in the Massachusetts city of Brockton in the wee hours of the morning of March 10, 1941. Shortly after midnight on that cold Monday morning, what appeared to be a routine fire was discovered in the cellar of the Strand Theatre in the heart of the city's downtown. Less than ten hours later, the twelfth body of a dead fireman was removed from the wreckage of the theater. More than twenty of his comrades lay in the hospital with injuries of varying degrees of severity. One of the injured would join his fallen comrades two days later, bringing the loss of firefighters to thirteen. Until the tragic events of September 11, 2001, this would rank as one of the largest losses of life suffered by firefighters in the collapse of a building in the history of the United States.

Thirteen husbands, fathers, sons and friends perished that morning doing what they loved, pursuing their duty with every ounce of courage and determination they had—brave men, heroes all, rushing in where danger called. The late nineteenth-century chief of the New York City fire department Edward Franklin Croker once remarked:

> *Firemen are going to get killed. When they join the department they face that fact. When a man becomes a fireman his greatest act of bravery has*

> *been accomplished. What he does after that is all in the line of work. They were not thinking of getting killed when they went where death lurked. They went there to put the fire out, and got killed. Firefighters do not regard themselves as heroes because they do what the business requires.*

So it was with John F. Carroll, Raymond A. Mitchell, William E. Murphy, Daniel C. O'Brien, Matthew E. McGeary, John M. McNeill, Henry E. Sullivan, George A. Collins, Denis P. Murphy, Roy A. McKeraghan, Martin E. Lipper, Frederick F. Kelley and Bartholomew Herlihy—the fallen, the heroes of the Strand.

The City of Brockton has never forgotten the sacrifice of these men. Each year, for more than three-quarters of a century, the city's firefighters and their officers, elected officials, descendants of those who perished and ordinary citizens—many not yet born on that fateful day in 1941—gather on March 10 to honor the fallen. A fitting memorial stands today near the still empty land on which the Strand Theatre once stood.

In this volume, the first account of the tragedy gathered in a single work, the authors have brought together many news accounts of the tragedy, including personal eyewitness accounts, some heretofore unknown; vivid and heart-wrenching photographs, most by noted Brockton news photographer Stanley A. Bauman; family remembrances of personal loss; and stories of the untold love of the citizens of Brockton for their fallen heroes of March 10, 1941.

1
Prologue

Brockton, Massachusetts, the men's shoe capital of the world, by 1907 had become the state's twelfth-largest city with a population of fifty-two thousand. Thirty-five shoe factories, composed of more than one and a half million square feet of floor space and employing more than fifteen thousand workers, dotted the urban landscape. By the end of 1907, seventeen million pairs of shoes with a value of more than $42 million were produced, and the payroll of the shoe manufacturers exceeded $9 million. With this burgeoning economy, factory workers were among the citizens enjoying leisure time and seeking entertainment. Theaters were popping up around the country, featuring a mix of the familiar vaudeville acts along with a relatively new genre of entertainment, the motion picture.

At the beginning of 1907, Brockton had three theaters and room for more. When the F.B. Washburn bakery vacated its location on School Street, theater entrepreneur Michael Sheedy, a Connecticut native who operated a string of theaters in Rhode Island and Connecticut, leased the property from Merton Gurney and his brother, Sanford, and the heirs of Francis B. Washburn to convert the building into a theater. Sheedy hired T.F. Hynes of Fall River, Massachusetts, to manage the construction aspects of the project. Standing at the site with Hynes on September 15, Sheedy stated, "There's the property, now go ahead, when can we open?" "December twenty-third" was the laconic reply.

With the exterior structure in place, the majority of work was concentrated on the interior. There would be a narrow entrance opening onto Main Street, but the theater's main entrance would be on School Street. The building was nestled among many newer and taller buildings with no façade visible from the street. The new School Street entrance would be a long arcade measuring sixteen feet, nine inches wide, and was designed to replicate the subway entrance to the Boston Theatre with a white colonnade highlighting dark-red walls and robin's egg–blue ceiling panels. The theater was designed to seat nearly eight hundred patrons in a space likened by many to Boston's luxurious Majestic Theatre. Sheedy's playhouse would have four boxes on either side of the house, each seating four. These boxes were highly ornate in design, cream in color and furnished with chairs made of willow. Leather seating filled the auditorium, and a heavy, deep-red Brussels carpet covered the floor of the theater with the ceiling painted in watercolors giving a beautiful sky and cloud effect.

The proscenium arch was festooned with myriad tiny electric lights, and the entire house was operated from the stage. The stage featured four drops, large canvas curtains on which scenes were painted; these were rolled up to the ceiling and lowered when needed. This was a significant number of drops, considering that the country's largest theaters had no more than six. These drops were designed and produced by Carmine Vitolo of Fall River, an artist Sheedy used in his other houses. The drops consisted of scenes of a garden, a woodland setting, a street and an interior. The theater had its own orchestra, with Max Zunde as its musical director and violinist and W.F. Burrell as pianist. The *Brockton Daily Enterprise* announced that the theater had a multitude of emergency exits on three sides and "conforms to the state fire laws in every detail." Behind the stage was a one-story addition that held dressing rooms, storage facilities and a room for the security guard.

As December 23 approached, work on the theater was wrapping up. Hynes had met his goal, but to be safe and attend to last-minute details, Sheedy waited until 8:15 p.m. on Christmas Eve, December 24, 1907, to officially open the doors. Then, under a vast array of incandescent lighting that illuminated employees dressed in uniforms of light brown and gold, with brown braids and collar points emblazoned with a gold *S*, the theater opened. To celebrate the opening, Sheedy scheduled four shows for Christmas Day, following with a regular schedule of two shows a day.

While under the control of Michael Sheedy, the theater was managed by William A. Bullivant, a young man who later would serve the city as an alderman and mayor. Sheedy subleased the theater to Cunney & Hodgkins of Boston, and it in turn leased it to H.A. and Elmer S. Taylor of Providence, Rhode Island. In October 1913, Sheedy lost the lease on the theater, and it was passed to John W. Sullivan of Brockton and John L. Sullivan of West Abington, the latter being known as the "Boston Strong Boy," world champion bare-knuckle boxer. The lease was for a term of thirty years. The theater opened under Sullivan's management as the Empire Playhouse.

The Sullivan team ran a good house, and by all accounts, the Empire prospered, as did Brockton. But clouds of war were gathering in Europe. World War I broke out on July 28, 1914, with the assassination of Archduke Franz Ferdinand of Austria. Soon the newspapers ran stories of the conflict on a daily basis. The war in Europe became a boon to the Brockton shoe industry, as many countries sought large quantities of boots and shoes for their militaries. Headlines throughout 1914 and into the spring of 1915 told of the growing conflict and the increasing production within the shoe factories of Brockton. Headlines changed from the war on Easter Monday, April 5, 1915, when the papers reported on a significant Easter Sunday blizzard. Subsequent editions spoke of the illness and eventual death of ex-governor of Massachusetts Curtis Guild at age fifty-five, the excitement over ex-president William Howard Taft's being in Brockton that week and the accomplishment of Jess Willard's seizing the title of world heavyweight boxing champion. On April 7, the headlines would scream, "Fire Destroys Interior of the Empire Theatre."

Shortly after 2:00 a.m. on April 7, 1915, four men standing in front of the Enterprise Building noticed a bright glow in the sky from the direction of School Street and sounded the alarm at Fire Alarm Box 34 at Main and Centre Streets. Arriving almost immediately on scene was captain of Squad A and First Assistant Fire Chief William F. Daley, who sounded a second alarm at 2:18 a.m. from Fire Alarm Box 21 on Main Street, and at 2:21 a.m., Daley sounded the general alarm. Officers George Drake and Carl Lind of the Brockton Police Department, which was located next to the theater, were sent to warn boarders in the adjacent buildings to evacuate. The iron shutters on the police station were closed to protect the glass from heat and to keep it from breaking. When crews arrived at the theater, flames were showing through the roof, and the entire interior was engulfed by the fire. The physical location of the theater made reaching the fire extremely difficult since the Empire was surrounded on three sides by buildings of greater height. Only the side of the theater facing City Hall Square was accessible. Fire soon spread to the adjoining Washburn Block and to the Builder's Exchange located on its second floor. Local business owners were notified of the conflagration so that they could respond to the fire to protect their property if need be. Night watchman Robert B.

Slesser narrowly escaped suffocation as he slept in the rear of the theater and was awakened by dense smoke. All five of Brockton's engine companies, its ladder companies and Squad A were on scene and had a dozen hose lines directed on the inferno, including some on the roof of the Washburn Block to prevent sparks and embers landing on other structures. Through the valiant efforts of the firefighters, the fire was contained to the theater and a small section of the Washburn Block.

The Empire was a total loss with the exception of some personal belongings of a visiting theater company that were salvaged. New stage drops, installed two weeks prior to the fire, and a new motion picture machine were all lost. The loss of property to the lessees was $1,000, and they were uninsured while the building loss amounted to $15,000, all of which was covered by insurance. The Builder's Exchange suffered some damage, as did the F.B. Washburn Company store, which had to destroy its inventory of baked goods and confections, all of which had been contaminated by smoke. Popular Main Street merchants Storey & Co., a women's clothing store, and Fraser's Dry Goods store suffered heavy smoke damage but were saved from fire by a twenty-inch-thick brick firewall. For weeks after the fire, both of these establishments ran large ads in the *Brockton Daily Enterprise* announcing discounted prices on merchandise damaged by smoke.

The Brockton police department protected the fire scene while local and state officials investigated the cause of the fire. Lessee John W. Sullivan and the stage manager were the last to leave the theater and reported that everything seemed in order when they left. Although many rumors persisted that the fire was the work of an arsonist or began in the projection booth, no cause of the fire was ever determined. Standing at the scene after the fire, J.W. Sullivan remarked to a reporter, "A large, more modern theater will rise from the ruins."

2

"A Great House"

Barely had the embers from the Empire cooled when plans began to be drawn up for a new theater. Should it expand closer to City Hall Square? Should it be taller? Should it be built? These were the questions of the day. There were those who had other building ideas in mind, such as constructing a covered arcade that would run from Main Street to city hall. As insurance claims were being negotiated, a goal was set to have a new house open as soon as possible at a cost of about $30,000.

Brockton architect William F. Barlow Jr. was selected to design the new theater. Barlow was a prominent architect of both residential and commercial properties, and his offices were located in the Bixby, a mixed-use commercial and residential building located at 80 North Main Street. Barlow was the author of the 1913 book *Ideal Homes*, a publication of over one hundred pages showing many home designs as well as commercial and industrial designs that he created. The primary directive that Barlow was given was to design the theater for "comfort and crowds."[1] The new theater would be known as the Strand Theatre.

Barlow would design a theater that could seat 1,685, Brockton's largest. The main entrance would remain on School Street to eliminate the need for a grand façade; however, the design was such that a Main Street entrance of elegant design could be added in the future. Barlow included many exits from the building. In fact, he had 20 percent above the state requirements for a theater with the seating capacity of the Strand. The Brockton contractors Powers Brothers began excavations of the foundation on August 4, 1915. The dimensional layout of the building would be 74 feet of frontage toward School Street, a rear width of 22 feet, a depth of 139 feet and a height of 60 feet.

The overall decorative color scheme of the theater would be rose and old gold. The proscenium arch would have a mosaic design in old gold, the stage walls would be finished in various tints of brown and rose and the building would have a buff ceiling. The walls of the house would be finished in a Turkish tapestry design of wisteria. As patrons entered the theater, they walked down an entry promenade of marble and tile with the walls showcasing posters of upcoming feature entertainment, from vaudeville shows to the latest motion pictures. At the end of the entryway, the ticket booth was the dominant feature. Finished in old gold and rose with leaded opalescent glass surrounding the top, the ticket booth contained the most up-to-date electrical ticketing machine available. From the foyer, two seven-foot stairways—carpeted in the same heavy rose-colored carpet of the aisles—led to the mezzanine level of the house, which was where the restrooms, resting rooms and business offices were located. From the mezzanine, a half flight of stairs led to the balcony. The main theater would seat 925, and the balcony would hold an audience of 760.

Incorporated into the design were some of the latest technological amenities of the day. All parts of the building were linked with an internal telephone system, and all exits were furnished with "panic bolts" capable of thrusting the doors open with the slightest touch. The house furnishings were constructed from Circassian walnut, which is today considered one of the most valuable and expensive woods available for cabinet and furniture construction. The seating in the orchestra section of the Strand was upholstered in leather. The theater's lighting was described in the *Brockton Daily Enterprise* as being an X-ray lighting system with huge inverted domes, artfully suspended from the roof, diffusing a pleasing light off the buff ceiling. In his book *On Building a Theatre*, acclaimed actor and director Irving Pichel would describe this X-ray lighting system as having mirror reflectors of whorled corrugations that would diffuse light over a large area, especially on flat ceilings.[2]

The Strand's stage was thirty-five feet deep with the proscenium opening being thirty feet wide and the stage having an overall width of forty-eight feet. Located under the stage were five dressing rooms for vaudeville performers, as well as room for expansion of dressing rooms and storage. The stage boasted $1,500 worth of scenes, including an interior setting, an exterior setting and a palace, as well as chamber and garden groupings, all designed by the Lee Lash Studios in New York. Establishing his studio in 1891, Lash grew it into the largest studio producing theatrical scenes in the country and is best known for his innovative use of real advertisements in scenery portraying street scenes. Lash also pioneered having a stock book from which theaters of all sizes could choose a design and provide their desired dimensions for the scene to be produced. By this method, Lash was able to serve the needs of all theaters, large or small.[3]

The theater was heated with a vacuum system of steam heat, which was quiet and efficient. This system provided direct heat through radiators and indirect heat through a modern blower and ventilation system. Large fans were concealed in ductwork that would circulate air from a fan room below the orchestra pit with an exhaust to the outside of the building. A forty-eight-inch ventilator and fan provided ventilation to the balcony at the rear of the theater.

In 1896, the first theater dedicated to showing motion pictures opened in New Orleans. Called Vitascope Hall, it was named after Thomas Edison's Vitascope projection machine. Thus began an entertainment industry that would grow rapidly, unbridled by regulation. In 1905, the Commonwealth of Massachusetts, realizing the boom in this industry, enacted its first regulations for the protection of its theatergoers. Motion picture film of this era, and in fact up until the 1950s, was nitrocellulose or nitrate film, a highly combustible material that was involved in many deadly fires in theaters around the world. Because it produced oxygen when it burned, nitrate film, if aflame, would continue to burn even when totally submerged in water. The Massachusetts regulation, chapter 791 of the Acts of 1914, was very specific in what the design and construction of the projection booths had to be, as well as in regulations for operators and more.

The very first section of this law addressed the issue of egress by stating that the placement of the projection booth should be such as "not to obstruct or render dangerous any aisle, passageway or egress. Proper access to the booth or enclosure shall be provided." The Strand was designed for three projection machines; therefore, by statute the projection booth had to be "not less than 12'0" in width x 8'0" in depth." Of the three machines, two could be picture machines and one a stereopticon. The latter was a holdover from the days prior to motion pictures when hand-painted slides were projected onto a screen and often referred to as magic lanterns. By the time the Strand was built, the major use of the stereopticon was for projecting advertisements on the screen.

The booth was to have an iron framework, the "walls and ceiling covered with asbestos wood or asbestos building lumber at least ¼" thick and the sheets so cut and arranged that there will be no vertical joints in the panels and that all the horizontal joints shall come over the strap iron." Bolts spaced no less than six inches apart were to fasten the asbestos panels to the framework. The floor of the booth, as well as the top of the rewind table, was also required to be of asbestos, with the subfloor being at least seven-eighths of an inch thick and screwed securely in place. The booth had to have two apertures for each projection machine, one six inches high and twelve inches wide for the projector itself and a second twelve inches high by six inches wide for the operator. If a stereopticon were used, it had to have a five- by five-inch aperture for the machine and the same size opening for the operator as the film projector. All of the apertures had to have

> *gravity slides set in metal runs...of galvanized iron, runs to be placed flush with the sides and bottoms of the openings and so formed that they will lap over the sides 1" on back and front....There shall be a special approved releasing device, with a fusible link inserted, within easy reach of the operator, by which the combustible cord holding the slides may be quickly released by hand.*

The door to the booth was required to be two feet wide and six feet high, fitted with iron overlapping the frame all the way around and fitted with a lock. The rewind bench was, as its name implies, where films were rewound after showing, and it was required to have two shelves made of slate or seven-eighth-inch boards painted with three coats of asbestos paint and covered in a quarter-inch-thick asbestos board. The bench could be no longer than four feet and no wider than a foot. The top shelf was for the rewinding equipment and process, and the second shelf was for the storage of films. There was a caveat in these regulations of which the Strand took advantage, and that was that rather than adhering to the regulations as written, the booth could be constructed of other, strictly fireproof material provided "that no such enclosure shall be erected until plans and specifications of the same have been filed with and approved by the inspector of the district in which it is to be erected." Located at the rear of the balcony, the Strand's booth was of terra-cotta blocks and cement and, at the time of the theater's opening, was hailed as the largest and most modern in the state. These booths were required to have ventilation on all sides and were to have galvanized pipes going through the exterior walls, controlled by dampers, to bring air into the booth from outside the building. The booth was also fitted with a twelve-inch fireproof flue going up through the roof of the theater with an electric fan inside.

The regulations included specific instructions on equipment set up in the booth and the wiring specifications for booths with projection machines having electric motors; many projectors at the time were manually operated with a crank. Each projector has to be bolted in place, and where more than one projector was installed, there had to be a clearance of three and a half feet between machines and a two-foot clearance from the walls. So dangerous was the movie film that every film was required to be stored in a metal canister with solderless seams and a tight-fitting cover. No smoking or matches were allowed in the booth, shut-off switches for all electricity within the booth had to be contained therein and a carbonic acid fire extinguisher had to be present at all times. The Acts of 1914 also included regulations pertaining to equipment operators. Projectionists had to be at least twenty-one years of age, take a written exam and pay a three-dollar fee for a license that was renewable annually for a dollar. Assistant operators had to be eighteen and were subject to the same exam. Interestingly, at the time, all of these regulations did not fall under the purview of the fire department but under the local police department, which was also responsible for the inspection of the building.

On March 6, 1916, Brockton's newest and largest playhouse was ready to open its doors to the public. On opening night, the theater, under the direction of manager John W. Sullivan, was crowded, and hundreds were turned away. Fire safety in the building was under the Strand's fire drillmaster, John J. Katwick, a former hoseman with Boston's Engine Company 11. Mayor John S. Burbank and members of city government were in attendance, as was William Bradley, the New England representative of the Triangle Film Company, whose film productions were being featured. In addition, Thomas Lannin, business manager of the Boston Red Sox, and Olaf Henriksen of the Red Sox were in the audience. Henriksen, the only Danish-born player to play in the major leagues, grew up in Wareham, Massachusetts, and later lived in nearby Canton. In 1908, he signed his first major-league contract with the Brocktons of the Old Colony League and had a fairly impressive career in this semiprofessional league until being bought by the Red Sox on August 10, 1911. Henriksen, an outfielder, would go on to play in the 1912 World Series and be an integral part of the Red Sox victory by driving in the tying run of the game. He was also one of the few players who would pinch-hit for Babe Ruth. Due to issues with Red Sox ownership, Henriksen was let go on June 30, 1917.

The opening show featured four vaudeville acts, nine reels of film and an eight-piece orchestra conducted by Clarence Fouche that filled the hall with music. The vaudeville headliner was the Shoy-Ling-Hee troupe, a group of Chinese performers and acrobats. A Keystone comedy film, *Crooked to the End*, featuring Fred Mace was shown, and the featured film was a popular Triangle Film Company production, *Peggy*, featuring famous actress Mary William Ethelbert Appleton "Billie" Burke. Burke would go on to star in the *Wizard of Oz* as Glinda the Good Witch of the North. Burke was also the wife of Florenz Ziegfeld Jr. of the Ziegfeld Follies. On opening night, the doors to the theater were festooned with floral tributes from the building's contractors. The house was complete except for final touches on a giant Hutchins pipe organ. This instrument featured a two-manual electric action and, true to theater organs of the period, a "toy box" consisting of sleigh bells, chimes, a snare drum, a bass drum and cymbals. Capable of imitating any instrument, including the human voice, the organ featured twenty stops and five thousand miles of electric wiring. Interestingly, the organ debuted on March 10, 1916, exactly twenty-five years before the tragic fire. The act "Jim Doherty and His Scotch Irish Lassies" were the first to perform with the instrument.[4]

The Strand opened with daily performances at two o'clock in the afternoon and continuous evening shows from 6:00 until 10:30 p.m. Admission prices were ten and fifteen cents with matinees being a dime and entry for children under fourteen a nickel. To celebrate its opening, the Strand hired the National Film Company to produce a film about Brockton. On March 24, 1916, this film was shot and featured each class of the high school marching out through the doors of the school and down the steps class by class. Various grade schools were visited and filmed, as were many factories and governmental and other public buildings. The film crew visited the police station and then the Central Fire Station on Pleasant Street, where they staged a response by the firefighters to an alarm. Upon completion, this film was shown at the Strand and then presented to city officials; however, no known copy of this film exists today.

For the next twenty-one years, the Strand operated as one of the city's great playhouses. In 1928, the Strand, along with the Washburn Block and other surrounding buildings, came under the ownership of Sanford K. Gurney and his sister-in-law, Ella P. Gurney, after they bought out other partners. The deal cost them $350,000. In 1937, the owners of the Strand property ended their lease with the Strand Corporation of Brockton, composed of S. Stone, Dennis I. Gorman of the Stone Leather Company, Henry I. Alexander of Alexander's Fashion Shop, Constantine Condikey, and with Alec H. Hurwitz as the house manager. The Gurneys leased the theater to Frederick E. Lieberman, president of Proven Pictures, an enterprise owning and managing many theaters within the Boston area. On May 22, 1937, Lieberman signed the lease on the Strand, which by this time was a house in disrepair as suggested in the wording of the lease:

> *The lessee…after the beginning of the term of this lease install at least one thousand (1000) new seats, new carpets where needed, all motion picture and sound equipment and whatever else is necessary to put the demised premises in first class condition to be operated as a moving picture theater, such as painting, decorating, drapes, drops, remodeling of the front of the theater, new marquee, etc. at a cost of not less than Fifteen Thousand ($15,000.00) Dollars….It is hereby understood and agreed*

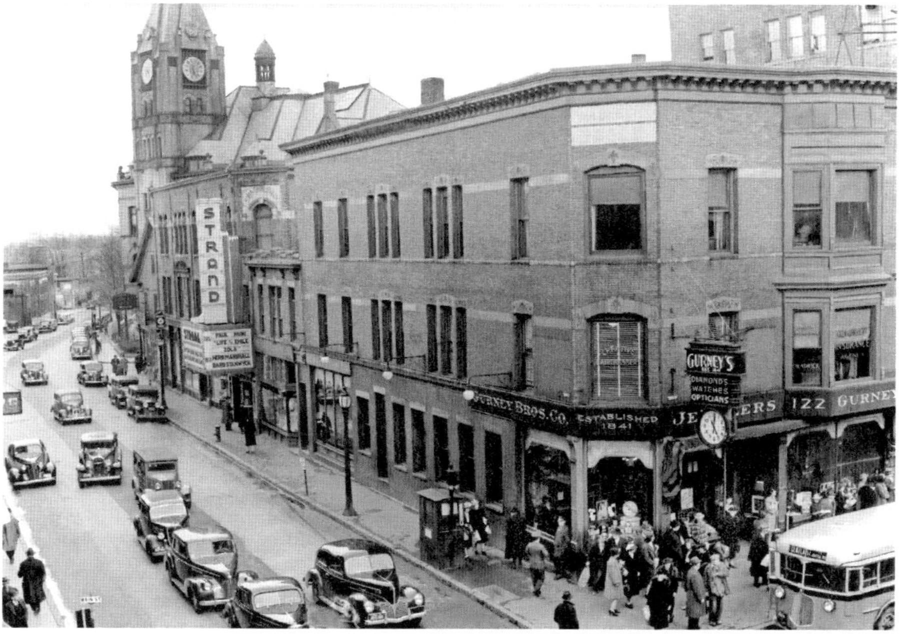

This 1937 photograph of the Washburn Block, at the corner of Main and School Streets, shows the new Strand Theatre marquee shortly after completion of renovations. *Bauman Collection, Stonehill College.*

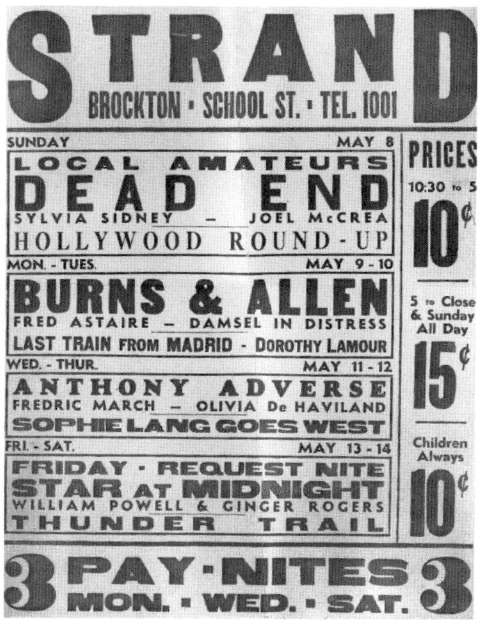

This poster from 1937 showcases a week's offering at the Strand Theatre. *Brockton Fire Museum.*

> *that the lessee may build a marquee over the entrance to the theater at #15 School Street....The Lessee may install a sign similar to that present* [sic] *installed on the roof of the Main Street Building.*

The August 16, 1937 edition of the *Brockton Enterprise and Times* announced that Lieberman would begin extensive renovations to the Strand immediately. In addition to the specific improvements required by the lease, others would include the installation of air conditioning and changes and improvements to the restrooms. Lieberman announced that he hoped for an October 1 opening and boasted that when complete the "theater will compare with any of the best theaters this side of Boston." Lieberman entered into an agreement with the Brockton Building Trade Council requiring that all of the workers involved in the renovations would be union workers, all of the theater employees would be union members and all employees would be residents of Brockton. The theater's unique new seating of wide leather seats with mohair backs reduced the capacity to 1,500 from the original 1,685. The house would have all new lighting, a new heating system, a soundproof ceiling and an enlarged projection booth. Lounge rooms with restrooms were added on the mezzanine level. Each lounge was adorned with four divans and six chairs of elegant design, and featured an open fireplace.

Lieberman hired Canadian-born William W. Adams to manage the renovated house. Adams immigrated to Brockton in 1908 with his parents and graduated from Brockton High School with the class of 1914. After high school, Adams spent time in Charlotte, Detroit, St. Louis and Columbus in the circus and carnival industry before returning to Brockton in 1927 to manage the Colonial Theatre. Running a bit behind schedule, the Strand Theatre reopened on Sunday, November 28, 1937, to great fanfare and celebration. A large parade was organized and began at Pleasant Street, marching its way south to Belmont Street, where it turned around and marched into the theater and across the stage. The Drum and Bugle Corps of Brockton Post 35 of the American Legion led the way, followed by a banner announcing, "We are on our way to greet Bill Adams, new manager of the Strand Theatre."[5] The marquee glistened with 360 lights, and theatergoers were greeted by usherettes dressed in military-style red jackets with blue stripes. The hall was adorned with floral tributes from other city businesses, politicians, contractors and well-wishers, and the Brockton Public Market sent a giant cake to be enjoyed by all. The opening-night audience, an invitation-only crowd, was treated to a showing of *The Trail of the Lonesome Pine*, starring Henry Fonda, Sylvia Sidney, Fred MacMurray and others. A second film shown was *Scarface*, featuring Paul Muni, Ann Dvorak, George Raft and others. The great house was again open.

3
"Water, Smoke and Fire"

In 1941, the city of Brockton, with an area of twenty-one and a half square miles and a population of sixty thousand people, ranked thirteenth in size among Massachusetts cities. Located around twenty miles south of Boston and twenty-five miles north of Providence, Rhode Island, the prosperous working-class manufacturing city, known for its thriving shoe industry, served as the hub for southeastern Massachusetts.

March 1941 was typical of a late New England winter, cold and wet with mixed snow and rain. Yet in many ways, it was anything but a typical March. Europe was at war, and the United States was on the edge, attempting to keep their distance but still supporting those whose political views they shared. On March 9, 1941, the German Luftwaffe once again bombed London, this time striking Buckingham Palace as well as the famous nightclub for the rich and famous, Café de Paris. At the café, a bomb went down a ventilation shaft, exploding in front of the stage. It killed thirty-four and injured at least eighty. World War II would be the last hurrah for Brockton's boot and shoe industry. But in 1941, shoe factories in the city of Brockton were busy filling orders for military boots and shoes for British, French and Russian troops. As war raged across the Atlantic, the conflict was on the minds of many Brocktonians. Daily newspapers filled with war news fueled residents' interests and concerns. Yet even as the war cast a long shadow of doubt and uncertainty, Brocktonians continued with their normal lives and routines, including attending movies in many of Brockton's theaters, not least of which was the Strand.

The city's fire department at the time was a highly dedicated and professional force with 123 paid firefighters operating five engine/hose wagon companies, three ladder companies and a specialized squad company from six fire stations. Firefighters were paid an average $35.40 per week for a regular eighty-four-hour workweek. However, firefighters were also expected to respond to all second and general alarms, even if they were off duty.[6]

The Alarms

On Sunday, March 9, 1941, the Strand Theatre featured the 1937 film *Hoosier Schoolboy*, starring Mickey Rooney, that had just been re-released. The second feature was the crime drama *Secret Evidence*, starring Marjorie Reynolds and Charles Quigley. Long after the moviegoers returned home, the Strand's night custodian, Christopher Moore, and his helper, Roger Thunert, were alone in the building cleaning up from the crowd when Moore discovered a fire in the basement area of the theater. Moore sent Thunert running to sound the alarm at Fire Alarm Box 1311 located at the corner of Main and High (now Frederick Douglass Avenue) Streets, a short distance from the theater. According to the entry in the logbook of Station 6 (the West Side Station, located at Belmont and Boylston Streets), the first alarm was struck at 12:38 a.m. on Monday, March 10, 1941. Dispatched to the scene were Engine Companies 1, 4 and 5; Ladder Company 1; and Squad A, a total of around twenty-three men, in addition to a deputy chief and aide. John Murphy, age sixty-five, was the deputy chief on duty that night. *Brockton Enterprise* night reporter Cornelius (Connie) F. Lyons was working that evening and sat quietly in the Brockton Police Station, located next door to the Strand Theatre, waiting for a story to develop.[7]

> *I was talking with Mrs. Alice Devine, police matron when the first alarm sounded. Jumping into the police ambulance with house officers I went to the fire scene. Upon entering the theater, I observed the firemen under Deputy Chief Murphy chopping a hole in the flooring on the left side of the main entrance to the matinee floor. Once the flames broke through smoke filtered through the theater to such an extent that Deputy Chief Murphy sounded a second alarm.*

That second alarm was sounded at 12:44 a.m., only six minutes after the first alarm. Responding to the second alarm were Engine Company

2, Ladder Company 2, Brockton Fire Chief Frank Dickinson, Deputy Chief Lawrence Lynch and all off duty members of the department. In 1941, off-duty firefighters had to be called by telephone to be notified to report for duty and were supposed to have a telephone in their residence. One firefighter, Allan A. Minnehan, who lived in a multi-family house on Baxendale Avenue above the LaLiberte family, relied on the LaLiberte's line to receive his calls. Alice LaLiberte, the twenty-year-old daughter of Emery and Mary LaLiberte, answered the call and notified Minnehan. An operator at the phone company, Alice was told to report to work. Minnehan did not have a car and asked for a ride. Alice's younger brother Joe drove both her and Minnehan to downtown Brockton since their father was away. Arriving on Main Street near the theater, Minnehan exited the car and headed to find his company while Alice headed to the phone company. Joe LaLiberte recalled in an account of the fire, "I later learned in the excitement of the moment, the car was left still running, and it stayed there in the middle of Main Street until it ran out of gas."[8]

Captain Patrick F. Stack of Engine Company 1, who arrived at the scene after the first alarm under Deputy Chief Murphy, in a rare interview with the *Brockton Enterprise* described the scene as follows:

> *When we went down we laid a line from the hydrant in front of the main entrance. As soon as we got in there we threw three to four cellar pipes* [a cellar pipe is an appliance for shooting water to all parts of a compartment under a floor or ceiling] *to all parts of the cellar below the floor in front of the entrance. We killed the fire in the cellar on that particular spot. The fire was working up through the south and west walls. The lines were then taken to the first balcony* [mezzanine level] *by the men of the first platoon, Henry E. Sullivan, Denis P. Murphy, Martin E. Lipper and George A. Collins.*[9]

Arriving on the second alarm, Captain John Carroll entered the theater with his men, wearing his black helmet, the front emblazoned with the captain's white shield and a large numeral "3" for his ladder company. A "fireman's fireman," Carroll moved forward, toward the balcony, calling to his men, "Come on, boys!" as he led them through the darkened theater, filled with acrid smoke and building heat. With the smoke and fire growing in intensity and moving upward through the building, Deputy Murphy sounded the general alarm at 1:19 a.m. (although some newspaper accounts attribute the general alarm to Chief Frank Dickinson), bringing all of the

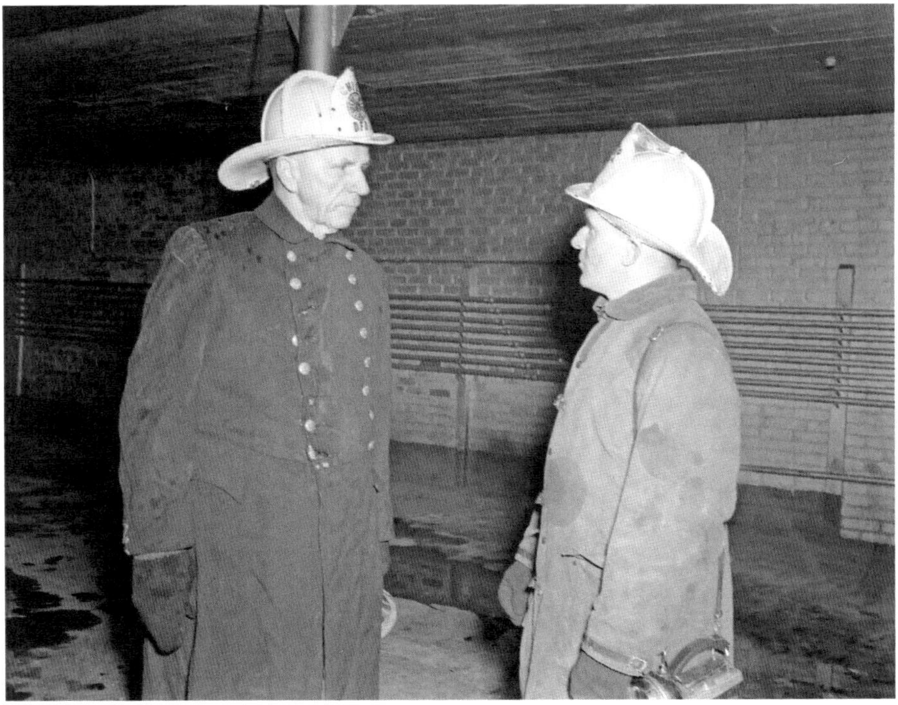

Brockton Fire Chief Frank Dickinson (*left*) and Deputy Chief Lawrence F. Lynch confer in the police station garage next to the theater on March 10, 1941. *Bauman Collection, Stonehill College.*

city's firefighting resources to the scene, including over one hundred men, five engine companies, three ladder companies and a specially trained squad company, Squad A. Additionally, aid was called for from West Bridgewater, Abington and Stoughton to respond to the fire scene and to cover vacant stations. When all of the apparatus had responded to the general alarm, the streets were clogged with all available means to quench the flames. On School Street, Engine Company 1 set up four lines, joined by Squad A, Combination 1, Combination 4 and Engine Company 4. Ladder 1 was positioned in City Hall Square, and farther down on School Street were ambulances and Engine Company 2 with three lines aided by Combination 2. On Main Street, according to former Fire Chief Burrell, Ladder Company 2 raised its eighty-five-foot wooden aerial ladder to the roof of the Kennedy Building. Engine Company 5 ran three lines; Ladder Company 3, Engine Company 3 and Combination 5 ran one line along with an engine company from Stoughton. In all, fourteen two-and-a-half-inch hoselines were used to try to subdue the flames.

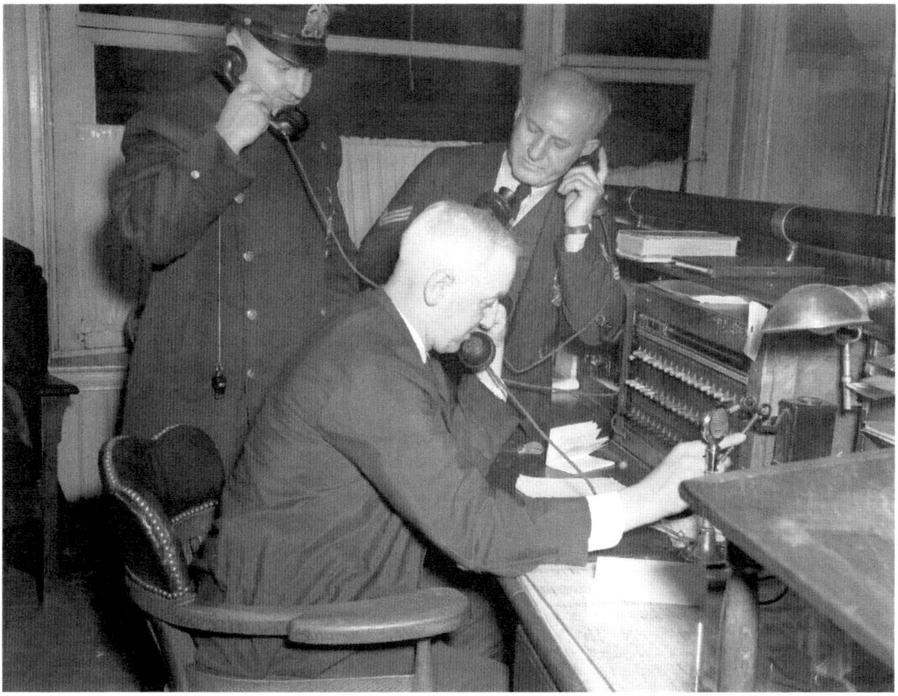

A look at the Brockton police station switchboard that fielded hundreds of calls on the night of the Strand Theatre fire on March 10, 1941. *Bauman Collection, Stonehill College.*

Stanley A. Bauman, a photographer for the *Brockton Enterprise*, was awakened shortly after the second alarm was sounded by a phone call from Clarence J. Erving, who was manning the police department switchboard. Bauman recalled in an *Enterprise* article shortly after the fire: "The phone rang, half awake, I answered (and the voice on the other end said) "Big fire at the Strand Theatre! Double alarm!" Bauman, who had returned earlier in the evening from North Conway, New Hampshire, debated whether or not to go to what appeared to be a routine fire. Thinking that he still had all of his photographic equipment packed, he decided to go and see what was happening. Bauman estimated he arrived about six minutes after receiving the call, about the same time that men and equipment responding to the second alarm did, and observed heavy smoke in the rear of the Fraser Building. In an article published in the *Brockton Enterprise* the day after the fire, Bauman described the scene in detail:

> *I mounted the stairs of the Gurney building to the fire escape directly in back, talked to Bill Fencer and his nephew, Horace. Horace it seemed had*

been sleeping in the Gurney building room just ten feet across from the Strand and so I snapped a shot of him pulling hose through his bedroom window. Up until now it was still a routine fire and we were looking around for some newsy angle.

Bauman left Fencer's room and made his way to the theater, meeting Paul Keith, son of former Brockton mayor Roger Keith, on his way. Keith offered to help Bauman with his equipment, and the two of them entered the smoke-filled theater. Bauman recalled, "Yes there were pictures. Firemen in clusters of four and five struggling with hoses right in the center of the floor, amid the seats....The only drawback, I said to Paul, was the smoke. Even the slightest smoke fogs a picture negative so thoroughly that figures blend into the gray background."

While firemen directed their hoses at the balcony, walls and ceiling at the back of the theater, the stage became an observation platform for news

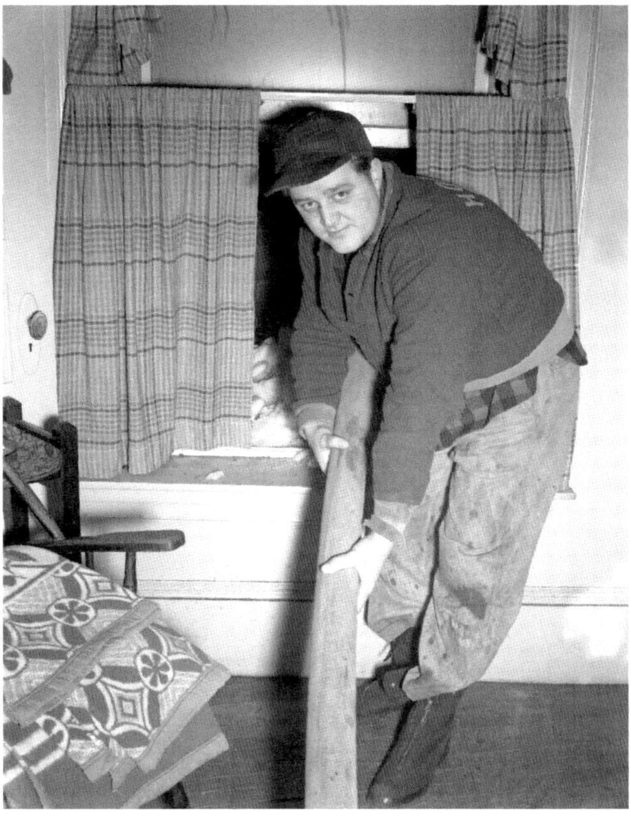

Horace Fencer, Gurney Building caretaker, pulls a hose through his bedroom window, just ten feet across from the Strand Theatre. *Bauman Collection, Stonehill College.*

reporters, sparks (fire enthusiasts or buffs) and plain citizens. Among those on stage were *Enterprise* night reporter Connie Lyons, city councilor John Asiaf, Mayor Fred D. Rowe and seventeen-year-old *Enterprise* newsboy Joseph "Joe" LaLiberte (who had driven firefighter Allan Minnehan to the fire). In a personal recollection of the fire, LaLiberte wrote, "I left my bed and home, and as I half dazedly rode towards that red glow in the sky, I never realized that that glow was soon to be made still redder with the blood of our firemen. I arrived at the fire and stood by the stage door…and watched in pride, the way in which our boys were fighting those flames." By this time, City Hall Plaza was packed with over one thousand citizens watching the fire.

Bauman and Keith, meanwhile, had been moving in and out of the theater attempting to find opportunities for newsworthy photographs. Slipping and sliding on the sidewalks outside the theater, as the water from the hoses froze, they made their way back inside to join the other onlookers on the stage. The firemen continued to direct hoses at the ceiling and walls with the water cascading back down over them. "The flames are breaking through the roof!" someone inside the theater hollered out.

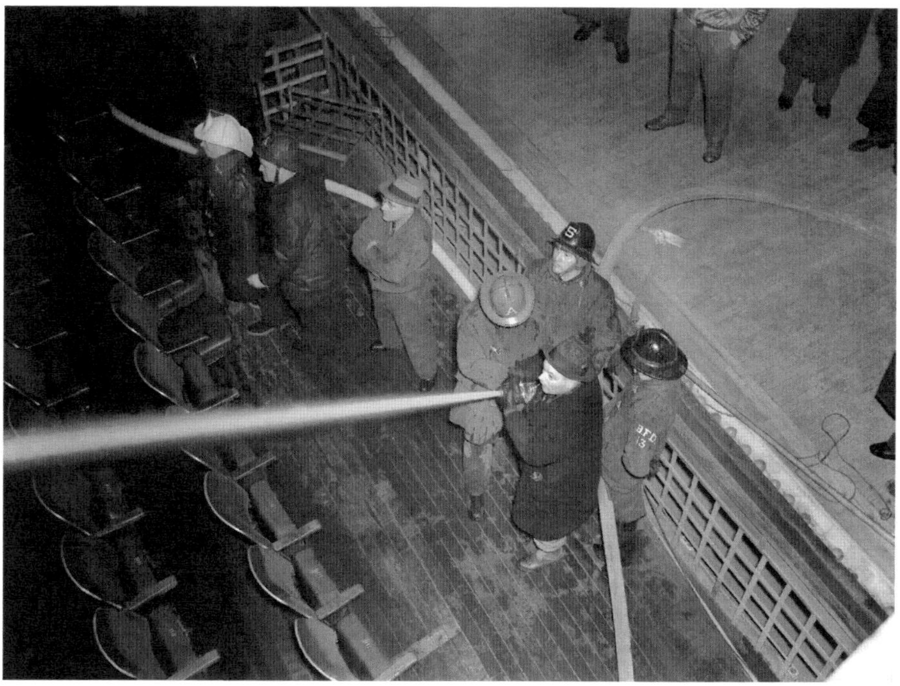

Taken from the balcony before the collapse, this photo shows firefighters and civilians directing a hoseline toward the balcony from the stage area. *Bauman Collection, Stonehill College.*

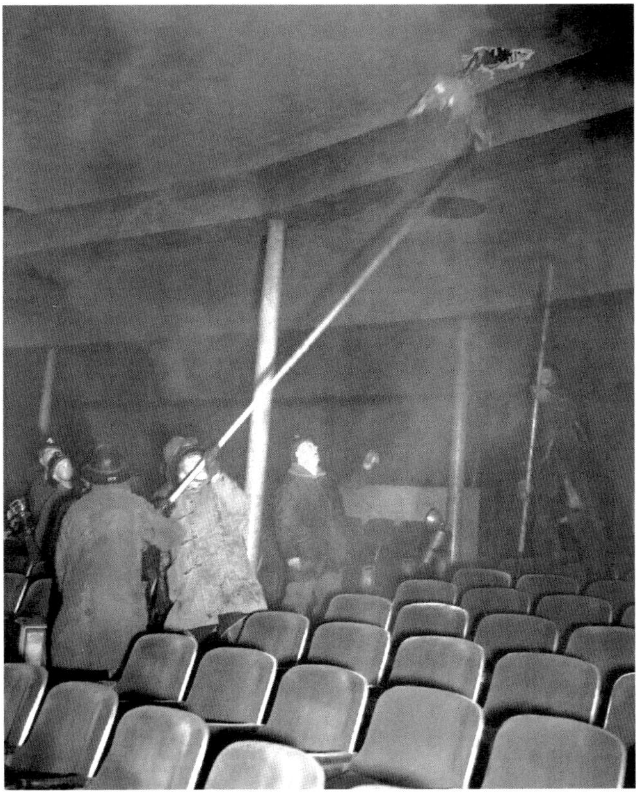

Firefighters faced the difficult task of trying to break through the wire lath and plaster ceiling to fight the fire. *Brockton Fire Museum.*

What seemed to everyone to have been a mere cellar fire had grown to a major conflagration, with fire inside the walls throughout the building, from cellar to roof. Men were on the balcony and under it working with ceiling hooks to pull down the ceiling to get at the flames. This proved to be an arduous task since the theater's walls and ceilings were plaster on top of wire lath. Wire lath was introduced in the late nineteenth century as an alternative to wood lath on which to apply plaster. Used mainly in commercial applications, the metal lath added strength and rigidity to a plaster ceiling or wall, as was the case in the Strand.

As firemen worked feverishly at pulling down the ceilings and running hoselines, Bauman and Keith moved quickly to the outside of the building, where Deputy Murphy was directing his men to train a stream of water on flames that were showing through the corner of the roof. In his March 10, 1941 *Enterprise* article, Bauman recalled that he looked around and saw a ladder leaning against the fire escape. He recounted the conversation with Keith at the fire in the article:

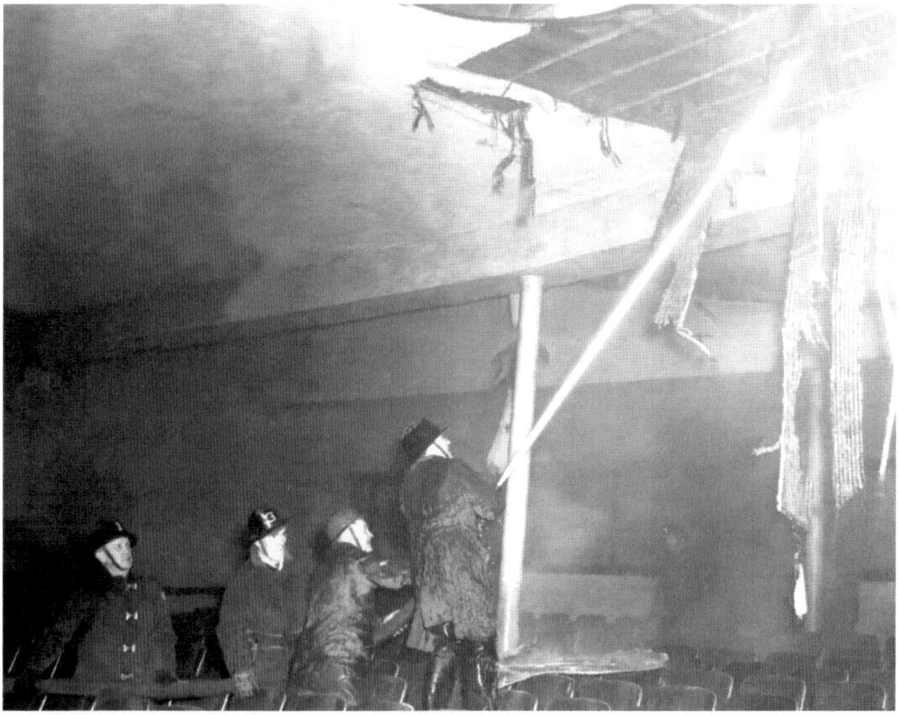

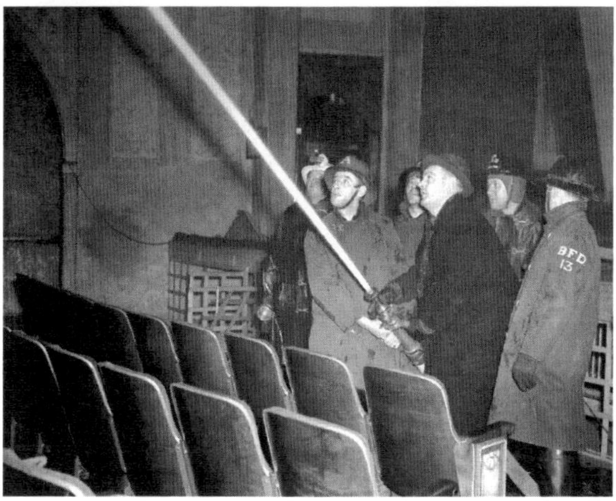

Above: Having opened the ceiling, firefighters direct a hoseline into the fire in the ceiling. *Bauman Collection, Stonehill College.*

Left: Firefighters and civilians in the orchestra pit direct water toward the balcony. *Bauman Collection, Stonehill College.*

"We're going up there." "O.K. by me" [Keith] *answered and we climbed the slippery ladder to the fire escape.... "Look out for that wall" deputy Murphy shouted, but we didn't think the wall looked weak and there wasn't much fire. Paul and I went back inside—on the balcony—and took a shot looking down on the firemen who were directing water towards us. We*

This photo shows the view of the fire breaking through the southwest corner of the building. Taken just moments before the collapse, there was no time to warn firefighters inside. *Bauman Collection, Stonehill College.*

> *joked with the newsmen on the stage below. Then out on the balcony* [fire escape] *again shooting toward the outside flame that just now began to break through.*

Even though fire was moving through the building, the sense among the spectators inside and outside was that things were under control, and many began to head for home thinking the worst of the fire was over. *Boston Post* correspondent Joseph R. Noone had been up under the balcony watching the men working the ceiling hooks and decided to join those on stage. Wading through ankle-deep water in the orchestra pit, he reached the stage. Noone recalled, "I was only casually impressed by the bantering vein adopted by a mixed audience of newspapermen, city fathers (past and present), and other spectators which was aimed good naturedly at Photographer Stanley A. Bauman, who was at the southeast wall of the balcony, taking numerous pictures of the daring firefighters."

THE COLLAPSE

As Bauman turned to re-enter the building with Keith, before he could re-load his camera, the roof came crashing down on the balcony "where only a little while before we saw those men. 'My God' I yelled to Paul as the wall shook beside us, 'there are firemen under there! This is awful!'" Joe LaLiberte recalled:

> *Suddenly, a yell rang out.... "The south wall is buckling." We drew back and waited. Then, with a deafening roar, the supports gave way, the wall split, and the wall and the roof fell.... We were horrified when we heard above the crackling of flames the agonizing screams of burning and dying men.... The stage door was flung open, a blood covered fireman staggered into the street, yelled, "There's about twenty of them trapped up there, for God's sake get them out!" He then fainted into the arms of helpful civilians.*[10]

Other accounts describe two separate crashes that occurred within minutes of each other. Captain Stack recalled Henry Sullivan, Denis Murphy, Martin Lipper and George Collins had been ordered to move from the first (mezzanine) to the second balcony. A matter of seconds after they got to the second balcony, the roof crashed in.

> *I had gone to the platform exit on the way to the Washburn building to see and check on the progress of the fire through the roof at the north wall. All this was in the pitch black except for light from the roof. I went out and heard the bricks clattering on the platform. When the roof let go we rushed into the first balcony to rescue men we feared had been trapped.... There was another crash and we rushed to the platform exit. When things quieted down we reentered the first balcony to look for men we feared were trapped.*[11]

When Captain Stack and Captain Herbert B. Gullefer of Engine Company 5, who was with him, reentered the first balcony, they found the stairs to the second balcony blocked by debris. Also looking for survivors were Courtney Simpson of Engine 5 and Deputy Chief Chester C. Smith of Stoughton. They told Stack that they had heard a cry for help. "Tracing the call," they found Bartholomew Herlihy of Ladder Company 1, who had been carried down to the mezzanine from the second by falling debris. Herlihy was brought from the wreckage and transported to the Brockton Hospital.

The rescue of George Maloney of Ladder Company 3 was reported by Noone in the *Post* that morning. "I saw the ceiling of the Strand Theatre suddenly collapse as more than two score firefighters, in the most shocking drama I ever witnessed, were buried under tons of debris. A flame seared ceiling gave way, literally to smash some of its unsuspecting victims through the balcony floor to the orchestra seats below."[12] Among those driven through the floor of the balcony by the falling debris was George Maloney of Ladder Company 3. Immediately after the collapse, newspaperman Lyons and Councilor Asiaf jumped from the stage and ran toward the balcony to give what aid they could. Seeing legs dangling from a hole in the balcony, the pair rushed to the aid of Maloney. Lyons recounted, "Standing on a seat I grabbed hold of him and as I did the seat tilted and we both tumbled in a heap on the floor." Lyons and Asiaf then carried Maloney to the Brockton police station next door, where he was placed in an ambulance and taken to the Brockton Hospital. Miraculously, Maloney survived, and the *Brockton Enterprise* reported he was treated at the scene and released. However, in reality, he suffered severe back injuries that would take more than two years for him to recover from.

Two firefighters with Maloney on the balcony when the roof came down were Andrew Johnson and William Lipper. The three were waiting for a hose to be brought to them. Johnson described in an interview with Brockton cable television's Barry Allen that the roof made a "whoosh" as it came down. A partition near the side of the balcony deflected most of the roof from the three firemen. Johnson tried to make it through the debris to the roof but was driven back by fire. He crawled out through a hole in the partition and jumped through the balcony floor to the seats below. The radio announced that Andrew Johnson was one of the firefighters who had been killed when in fact he was resting at home, having been released after treatment from the Brockton Hospital. The *Enterprise* also reported that he returned to the scene to search for his helmet that he had lost in the cave-in, but the newspaper did not say if he found it.[13]

Noone, unaware that Bauman had left the balcony, thought the worst for his friend and Bauman's aide, Keith. "I was certain that he had been buried in the wreckage along with his volunteer aide, Paul Keith." Noone ran from the theater, heading for a telephone in the police station to make a call to his newspaper. Unable to access a phone in the bedlam that reigned within the station, Noone ran several blocks through icy streets to his office. As he turned from City Hall Plaza onto School Street, Noone ran directly into Bauman, whom he described as "unscathed but visibly shaken." Upon returning to police headquarters, Noone saw firemen lying on the floor badly injured and more lying in the women's detention area, where he observed a prisoner gazing with unspoken horror at the form of an unrecognizable man on a bed a few feet away. Noone ended his story that frightful day with these words: "I believe the cries of those poor, unfortunate heroes will never leave my ears."[14]

Perhaps the most dramatic rescue of all was that of Lieutenant John P. Buckley of Squad A. Stanley Bauman reported the following:

> *Mayor Rowe, I think had arrived by this time and had joined the group on stage but firemen warned that the whole building was liable to fall at any minute. "And when it does" Deputy Murphy shouted "that whole draft of hot air will sweep you before it." Yes, there was danger—we all knew, but we couldn't go. Because over there in the left hand corner near the very last seat, firemen were digging. They were digging with their hands and choking and frantically grabbing at red hot timbers and plaster. Why? Because under that pile, with red embers raining down, a figure sat upright. Just his head was visible. I wanted to picture him, but the smoke was like a fog. The best camera in the world with the most powerful flash wouldn't pierce that haze. "It's Lieut. Buckley" someone said. "And there are others buried beneath him." I knew Lieut. Buckley well, always cheerful, always friendly, always helpful. I thought of that other tragedy at Waldo Lake a year and a half ago when Lieut. Buckley risked his life to swim for hours in the lake diving for the body of Robert Burns. But there he was buried in debris, with a hose dangling down from the ceiling pouring gallons of ice cold water over his body. Water, smoke and fire. That was the hell he had to go through. And through it all he talked with his rescuers. Yes, he talked with them and told them how to lift this board and that. I wanted to get this picture—the picture of pictures—but the smoke was too bad and firemen forbade any closer approach. Surrounding Buckley in the debris were the lifeless bodies of Captain Carroll, William Murphy and others. As Father Lawrence Morrisroe came to Buckley's side he shook hands with the injured firefighter and gave him the last rites of the church. Buckley looked at the priest and said "Pray for me father, but don't forget the other fellows in there."*[15]

Also rescued was William E. Kelleher of Engine Company 1. Kelleher narrowly escaped death while high up in the balcony when the roof came crashing in. As a section of the roof came down by him, Kelleher grabbed

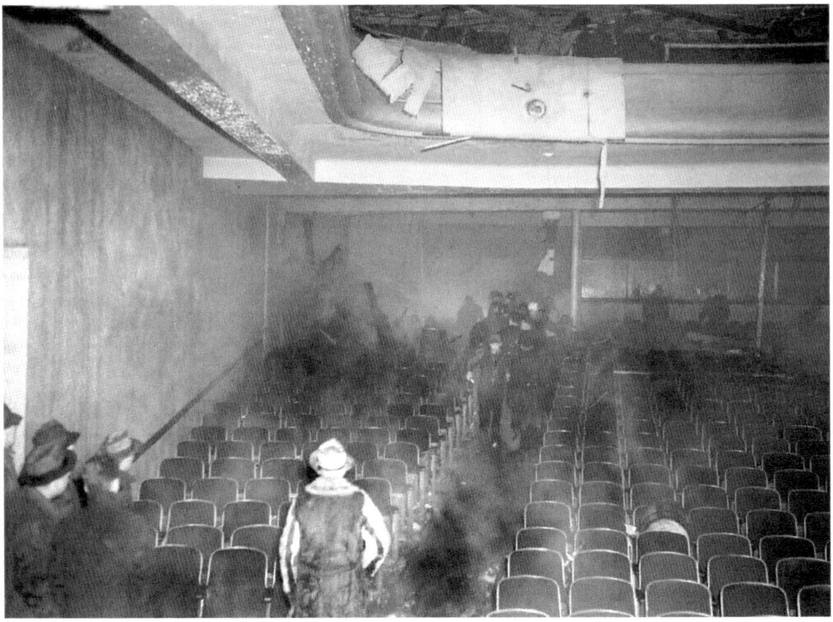

A firefighter looks on as others bring Lieutenant John P. Buckley, injured in the collapse, out from the debris. *Bauman Collection, Stonehill College.*

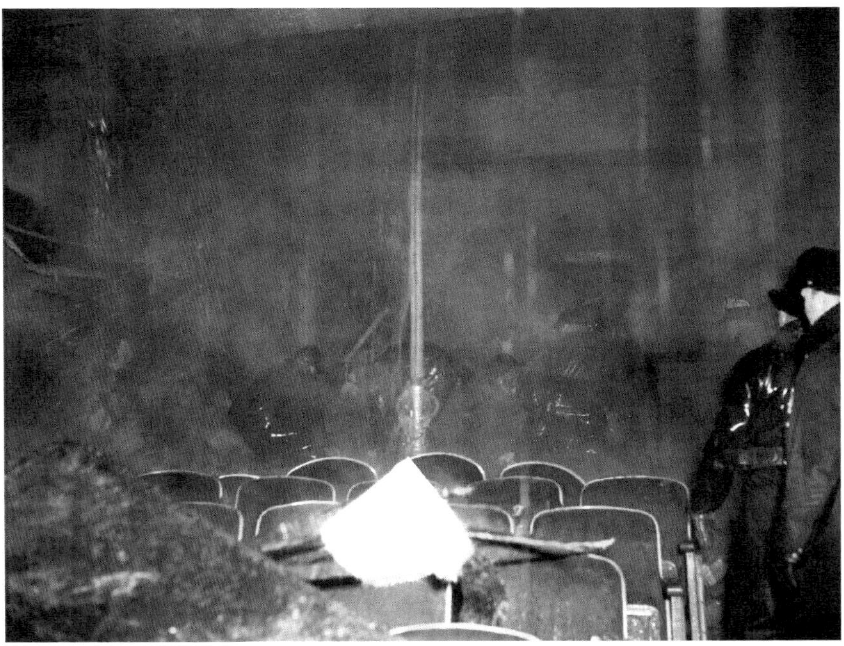

A hose hangs from the balcony, spraying water on firefighters in orchestra seats who were searching for survivors after the roof collapse. *Bauman Collection, Stonehill College.*

hold of roof rafters and was dangling precariously when local photographer Richard Crooker snapped a picture of the firefighter hanging in midair. With the roof, ceiling and fire below him, Kelleher dropped to the balcony floor, where Crooker and others led him from the theater. Kelleher was transported to the Brockton Hospital, where he was placed on the danger list after it was reported he suffered from a concussion and burns on his face and hands.

A stuck hose saved Lawrence "Larry" Johnson, a rookie hoseman with Engine Company 1, from serious injury or even death. As Johnson recalled in an interview on *Reminiscing*, a Brockton cable television show hosted by Barry C. Allen, Johnson and fellow firemen were pulling a hose line to the balcony when a fellow fireman called out, "'Larry, get the line its caught on the corner.' Just as I got to the head of the stairs the crash came, knocking me down the stairs and I was all full of debris. I was pulled out of the debris, Walter McClaren and Lt. Thomas Barron pulled me out." Chief Dickinson's driver, John Hamilton described Johnson's fall for the *Enterprise*,

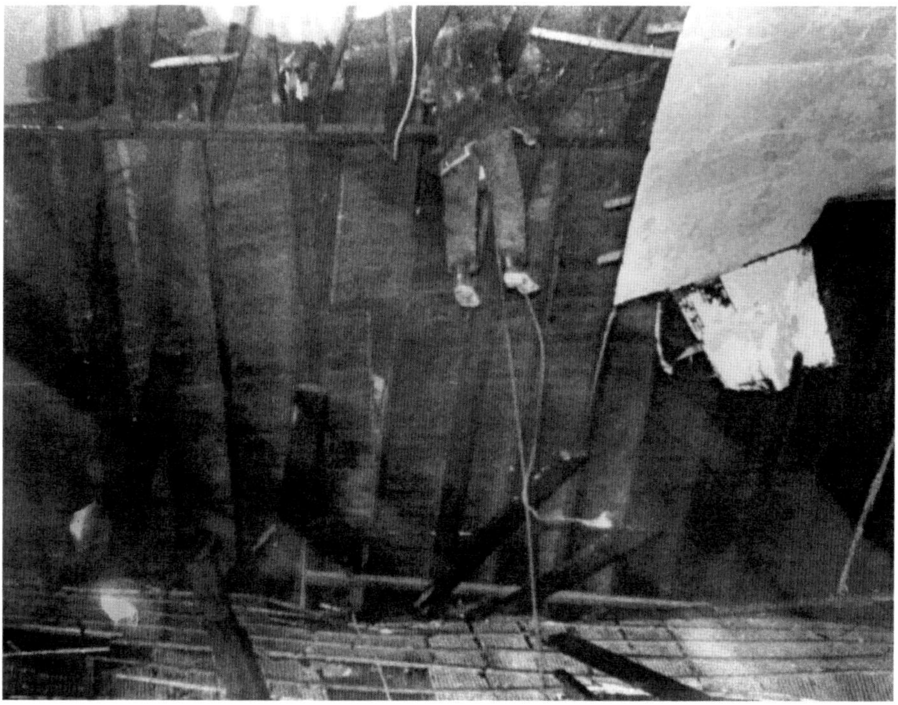

William E. Kelleher of Engine Company 1 narrowly escaped death when the roof collapsed by clinging to the rafters. Able to drop to the balcony floor, he was rescued and brought to Brockton Hospital. *Photo by Richard Crooker; courtesy of Brockton Fire Museum.*

saying, "Lawrence Johnson was pitched headlong and rolled head over heels down the stairway." Johnson, like other survivors, wanted to rush back in to help his brothers, and as Johnson recalled, he was told, "Don't go up there, it's bad, it's bad up there." Johnson would later say that when he did go up, "we saw hands sticking up and had to dig them out."

Also, escaping injury was Edward "Sonny" Burrell, a twenty-six-year-old newlywed who had been on the department for only two years when he received the call to the Strand. Assigned to Ladder Company 2 that night, his crew was sent to the roof of the Kennedy Building on Main Street, which backed up to the theater. The company's task was to lower a hoseline down into the flames. To accomplish this, company members were lowering a ladder onto the theater's roof when it collapsed. Five minutes' difference in timing and five more firefighters most certainly would have perished. In a 2008 interview with Milton J. Valencia of the *Boston Globe*, Burrell recalled that "all he could see was the crumbling metal and timber and smoke." Burrell recalled it being a cold night, but he kept spraying water into the theater because every time he stopped, he could "hear screams." He kept the hose going until the screams stopped.

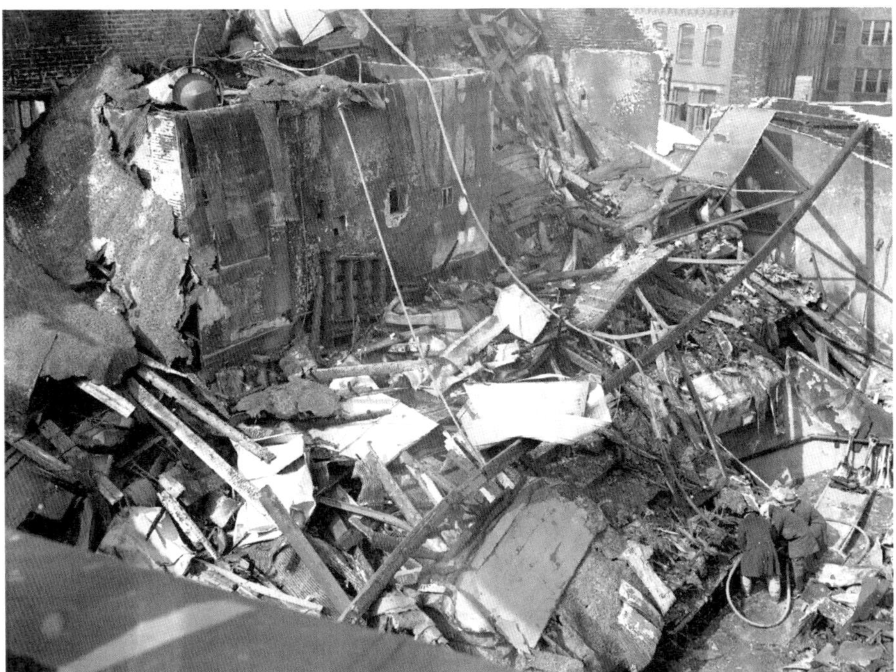

This view from the Kennedy Building of the collapse shows the buckled steel beam that is believed to have caused the roof collapse when it gave way. *Bauman Collection, Stonehill College.*

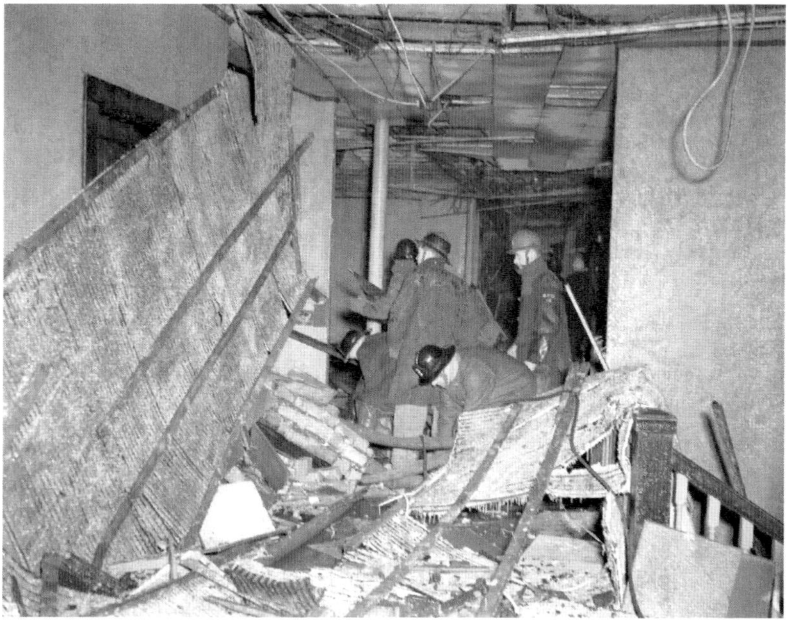

Firefighters search the debris for their trapped comrades. The bodies of three men were found in this wreckage. *Bauman Collection, Stonehill College.*

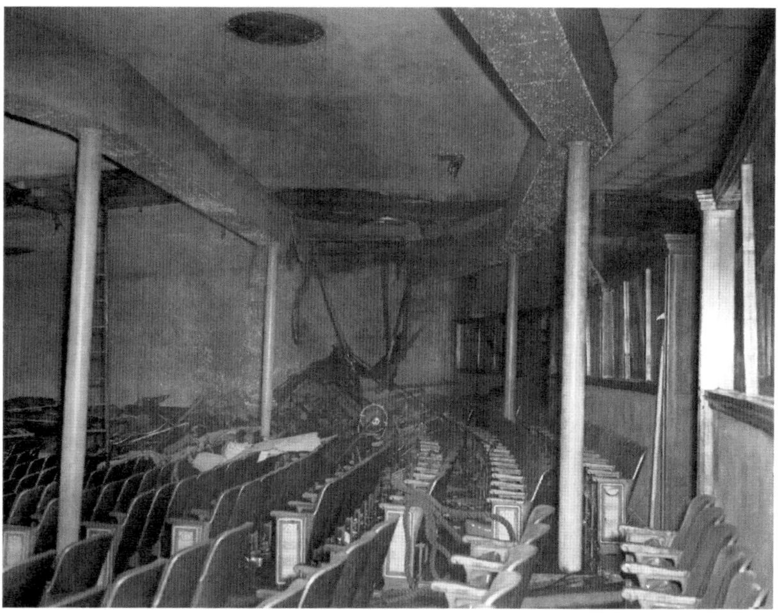

This photo was taken three days after the fire, on March 13, 1941, at the rear of the theater under the balcony and shows some of the damage from the collapse. *Bauman Collection, Stonehill College.*

Members of the building laborers' local were quick to volunteer their help to find the dead and injured. Herbert S. Ferris of the electrical workers' local and Victor Parziale of the laborers' local organized a rescue squad. The group included Ferris and Parziale along with Michael Tarentino, David DiCicco, Philip DiFalco, Louis Vacca, Harold Burke, Mario DiCarli, Sabino Mattoli, Eugene Willis, Joseph Allegra, Carl Crealese, John Kafantares, Mike Eovine and Joseph Manzini. Their knowledge of building construction was invaluable, and the *Brockton Enterprise* reported that "further collapse may have been prevented because of the cautions they took in moving the debris to get to the bodies."[16]

Outside the theater, members of the community did a yeoman's job of offering aid. A local insurance man, Fred Hendrick, had an office in the Washburn Block adjacent to the theater, and he opened the office during the fire as a place for firemen to rest and also to use the phone to call loved ones. Commanding officers took the loss of men extremely hard. Among those brought to Hendrick's office was Deputy Chief Lawrence Lynch, overcome by exhaustion and grief and nearly inconsolable. Lynch had fought long and hard for five hours beside his men to quench the inferno. The *Brockton Enterprise* reported, "By sheer force he was half carried, half dragged out of the building. He didn't want to quit. Not until his job was done. He became hysterical and his body shook convulsively. 'I should be in there with my men,' he shouted." Lynch, who one day would become chief of the department, was taken to Fred Hendrick's office, where he was attended to by Father Lawrence P. Morrisroe, the curate at St. Patrick's Roman Catholic Church. Father Morrisroe made his way through the unstable ruins of the Strand, administering the last rites of the church to the dead and dying. Father Morrisroe performed a similar task in the aftermath of Boston's Pickwick Club disaster when forty-three people died as the five-story building in which the nightclub was located collapsed without warning at three o'clock in the morning on July 4, 1925. Lynch was also joined by police sergeant Timothy O'Brien, who was assisting in the rescue but ordered out of the theater. O'Brien's brother Danny was among those still in the theater, but it was not known if he was among the dead. Concerned about his brother, the sergeant obeyed orders and joined Lynch. Looking at the shell-shocked deputy, O'Brien remarked, "Larry, what's the matter with you? Don't take it like this." Lynch looked back and responded, "I'd feel better about it…if I were under that pile with my men." O'Brien responded, "Suppose you were in my place.…My brother is still in there. Maybe he's—" Unable to speak further the two men gathered their thoughts and their courage and returned to the theater.

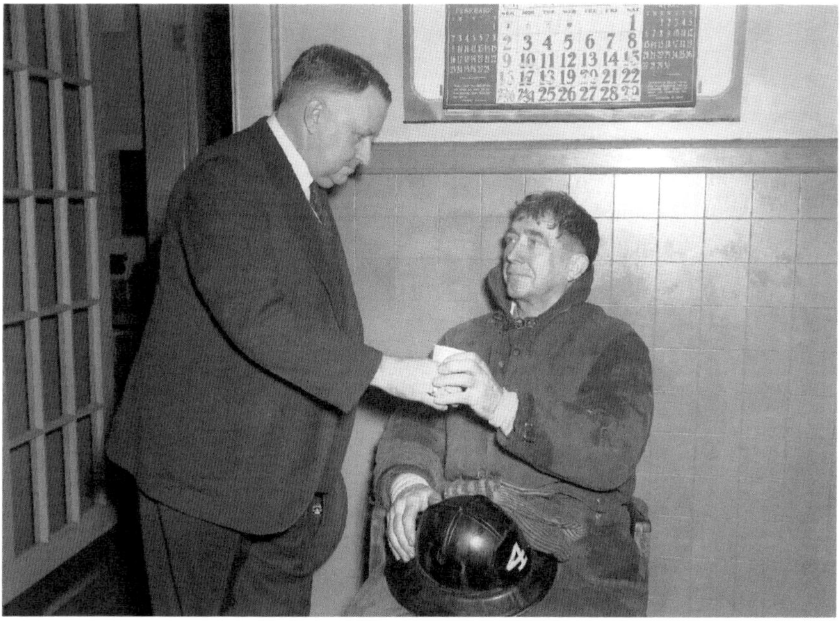

Mayor Fred D. Rowe was one of many at the scene to offer comfort and care to the exhausted firefighters. This photo shows him giving coffee to firefighter William Haverty, Engine Company 4. *Bauman Collection, Stonehill College.*

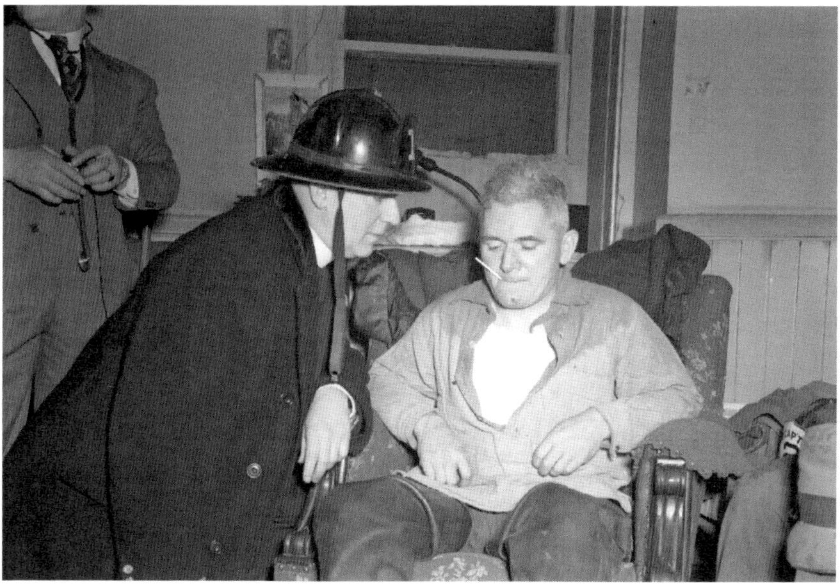

Donning a fireman's helmet to console and give last rites to those trapped in the fire, Reverend Lawrence P. Morrisroe, curate at St. Patrick's Catholic Church, comforts grief-stricken Deputy Chief Lawrence F. Lynch. *Bauman Collection, Stonehill College.*

The scene in Hendrick's office can only be imagined. Injured, exhausted men taking a break to have a smoke or shot of whiskey to calm their nerves, some waiting to be transported to the hospital for further treatment. A noisome concoction of sweat, blood, burnt flesh, waterlogged clothing, cigarettes and cigars all mingled with the haunting odor of smoke from the fire. It was the smoke that lingered, hanging over the office and the city, imbedding itself in the clothing, flesh and memories of the firefighters, reporters, sparks and onlookers. Hendrick's niece Alice LaLiberte, who had been working at the Telephone Office since the second alarm, recalled being relieved by the day shift. She had no idea what had transpired in the hours since arriving downtown. Looking for a ride home, she went to Hendrick's office. After entering the building, Alice made her way to the bottom of the stairs that led to her uncle's office, where she was hoping to find her brother so he could take her home. She had not heard of the collapse, and upon reaching the stairs to Hendrick's office, she was held back from ascending. LaLiberte reflected, "I didn't want to get up really. You could hear them screaming, there was a lot of pain going on in that office, but I didn't get up. I eventually walked home."[17]

Many firemen went to Hendrick's office to use the telephone to call their wives to let them know they were safe. Joe LaLiberte was in his uncle's office as the men came and went and gave this account of one fireman's phone call:

> *Towards morning, I don't remember the time, but it was dark outside, when a fireman, all covered with dirt and dust, and filthy of face and hands—one who had obviously been working heavily in debris—came into the office.... The fireman asked me if he could use the phone—"I'd like to call my wife and tell her that I'm all right—O.K.?" My uncle Fred standing nearby stated very matter of factly—"Of course—go ahead—call your wife." The fireman gave the number to the operator and waiting and while you could hear the phone ringing at his house. Suddenly the phone was picked up and a woman's voice could be heard "Hello!" The fireman quickly stated "I just called to let you know that I'm all right." He was, however, abruptly interrupted at that point with a female scream that could be plainly heard by all of us at that part of the office—"You mean," the female voice screamed, "You mean, that you woke me out of a sound sleep just to tell me that you were all right! I don't believe this—Me from a sound sleep and you just saying you are all right!" The fireman, now redden and almost scarlet of face—he looked around at all of us, who he realized had heard his wife's screaming. The fireman looked*

> *blankly at the phone in his hands, still saying nothing. He just stared at all of us for a moment or two and without comment slammed the phone back into its holder. He quickly left the office, muttering unintelligibly to himself as he headed down the corridor toward the second floor fire exit to the still smoking Strand Theatre.*[18]

The Brockton police station, located next to the theater, was turned into a first aid station and staging area for transporting the dead and injured. *Post* correspondent Noone recalled that the police station had become a "madhouse" after the collapse, as injured were brought from the theater.[19] Several city physicians arrived on scene to provide first aid, among them medical examiner Dr. Pierce Leavitt, Dr. H.J. Lupien, Dr. Bolis Asiaf, Dr. Edward Lagerstedt and Dr. Robert McGee. Captain Stack was treated in the police station guard room. Roy Franzen from the Franklin pharmacy, located in the city's Campello section, rendered first aid as well as provided medical supplies while Mayor Rowe and his brother, Judge William Rowe of the Brockton district court, directed efforts to transport the victims to the hospital. Massachusetts State Police arrived in downtown Brockton to aid in rescue efforts and to manage traffic in the area. The Brockton Gas Light Company also sent its first aid crews to assist. Shanley's package store, located in the block next to the theater, opened to provide firemen and rescue workers with whiskey to warm themselves and calm their nerves. The Embassy Club also provided quarts of whiskey. According to newspaper reports, local businessman Sam Shapira entered the police headquarters, looked around, left and returned with his arms loaded of cartons of cigarettes, and Schulte Cigar store also provided cigarettes and cigars. The Salvation Army, with doughnuts and coffee supplied by Asker's Bakery on Pleasant Street and the A&P Store on Belmont Street, supported the firemen both during and after the fire. After receiving first aid treatment, many of the injured firemen rushed back into the building in hopes of saving their comrades. Joe LaLiberte recalled injured firemen being led out of the theater begging, "I'm all right. I'm not hurt, lemme go back there, they need me…"[20]

The Brockton Hospital was a beehive of activity beginning at about two o'clock in the morning, when the first of the injured were brought in. Nurses and doctors, uncomplaining and with professional stoicism, attended to the injured and dying. As reported in the *Brockton Enterprise* on March 10, 1941: "After caring for the firemen the nurses couldn't sit down and relax. They had to clean up blankets, sheets, towels, bandages and

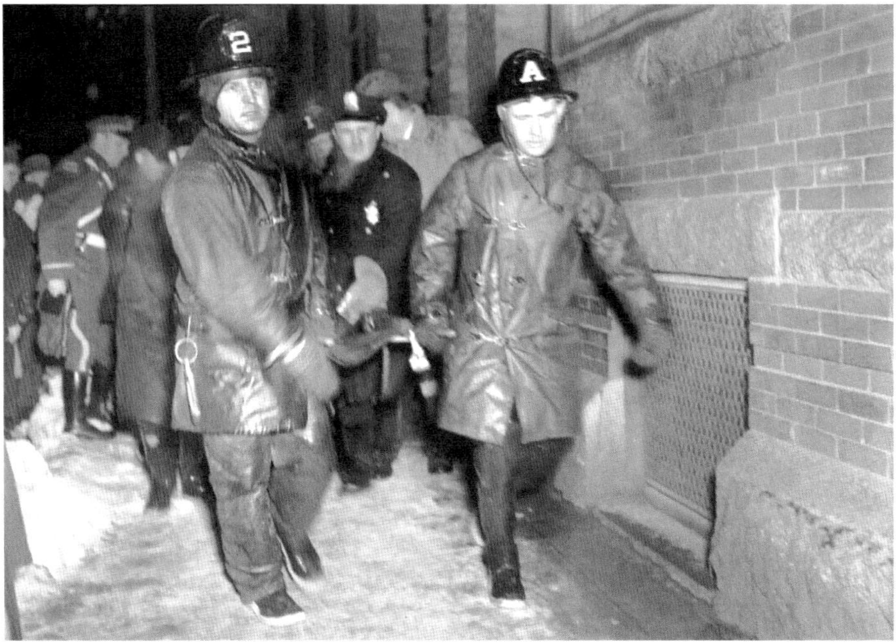

Firefighters and police braved falling temperatures and icy conditions to remove fallen comrades from the theater wreckage. *Bauman Collection, Stonehill College.*

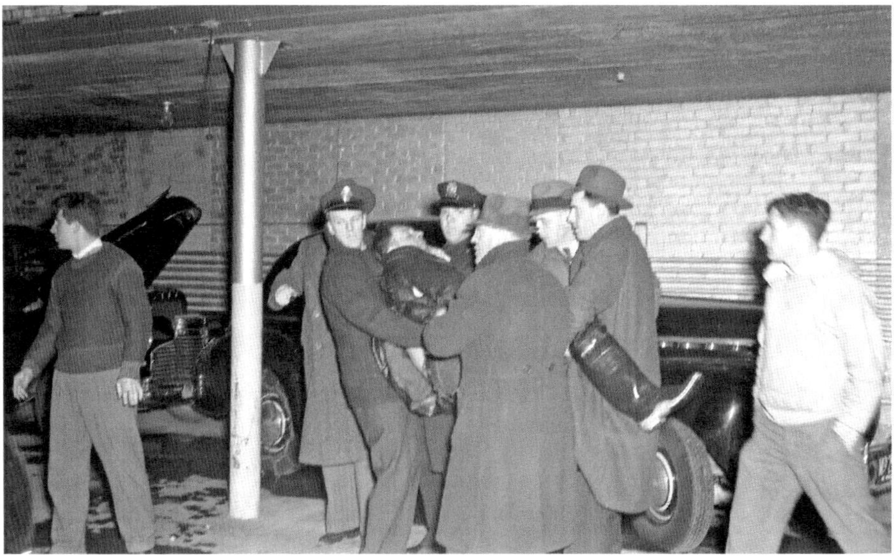

The police station located next to the Strand Theatre was set up as a staging area for the injured. This photo depicts an injured firefighter being carried from the theater to the police station before being transported to Brockton Hospital. *Bauman Collection, Stonehill College.*

immeasurable instruments." Dr. Loring B. Packard was kept extremely busy X-raying the injured. Many of the patients he saw suffered injuries from falling timbers and debris. Dr. Packard also X-rayed many firemen who complained of chest problems due to inhaling the toxic smoke from the burning movie film.[21]

Fearing that the walls and more of the roof could collapse Chief Dickinson ordered the building vacated, but at 6:00 a.m., the chief allowed men to once again enter the ruins to search for their brother firefighters, feeling that danger of further collapse was over. Because of the delay in removing the dead from the theater, the 6:00 a.m. extra of Boston's *Daily Record* newspaper, the first of any paper to carry the story, ran the headline "Fear 2 Dead, 12 Injured in Blaze." The bodies of Captain Carroll and William Murphy were the first to be removed from the wreckage. Carroll was a thirty-two-year veteran of the department, having been the driver of a hose wagon for Engine Company 4 when horses were still being used to haul apparatus to fires. Carroll was the fireman with the most years of

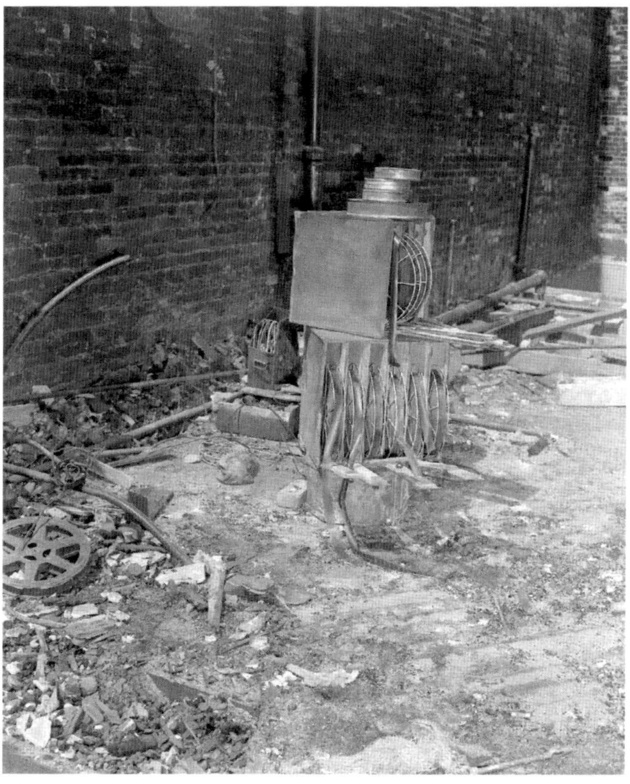

Burned film was at first believed to be the cause of the deadly fire, April 14, 1941. *Bauman Collection, Stonehill College.*

service to die in the fire while William Murphy, at age twenty-nine, had been a fireman for only four years, the least of any victim.

As the *Daily Record* hit the streets, bodies began to be brought from the theater, most of them unidentified. As each body was carried from the rubble, the procession would stop, and Father Morrisroe would administer last rites before the body was placed in an ambulance or hearse and brought to a local funeral home. Throngs of onlookers crowded the area around the Washburn Block to watch the grim march of the fallen. Axel C. Larson, the driver for the deputy chief, visited the undertakers attempting to aid with the identification of the charred bodies. Carroll and William Murphy were the only bodies not badly burned or disfigured.

At the Hickey Funeral Home, medical examiner Dr. Pierce Leavitt and Larson were able to identify Daniel O'Brien, Matthew McGeary, Roy McKeraghan and Lieutenant Raymond A. Mitchell. A fifth body at Hickey's was believed to be Denis Murphy. The bodies of Captain Carroll, Martin Lipper and George Collins were identified at the

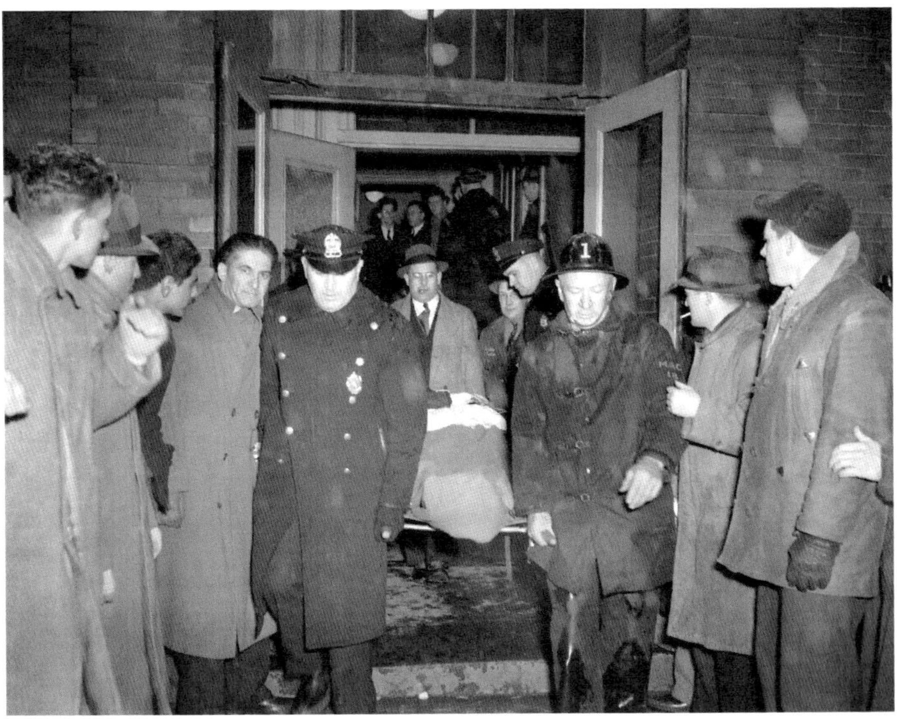

Police officer Ernest V. Emord (*left*) and an unidentified firefighter remove the body of a deceased firefighter from the ruins of the Strand Theatre. *Bauman Collection, Stonehill College.*

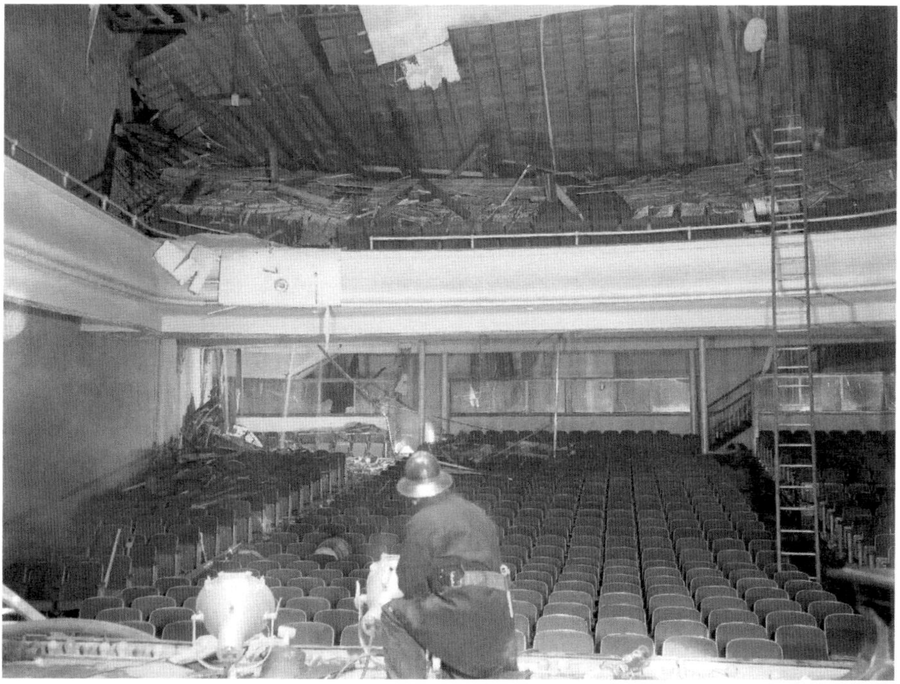

A grief-stricken firefighter surveys damage where his comrades were trapped and killed. *Bauman Collection, Stonehill College.*

McGlinchy-Russell Funeral Home. Lipper was identified by his stature and by wearing boots that were labeled M.E.L., and Collins was identified by a Hamilton pocket watch, a wristwatch, glasses and car keys. At the Conley Funeral Home, the bodies of William Murphy, John Malcolm McNeill and Henry Sullivan were identified. The last body to be removed from the theater was identified by Chief Dickinson's driver, Clarence A. Hamilton, as Frederick Kelley. Many of those killed were of Irish decent, with Denis Murphy having been born in Ireland. Most were Roman Catholic and men of deep faith. The families of all of the dead and injured suffered greatly. According to newspaper reports, many of those who had been on scheduled duty and were killed had phoned home earlier on Sunday to say hello to their wives and children, telling them it had been a slow day and that they would see them in the morning.

THE AFTERMATH

With the injured and dead accounted for by 10:00 a.m., less than twelve hours after the first alarm sounded, the city buzzed with hushed excitement. Hundreds of spectators crowded around the theater to see where friends, neighbors and family members died. Schoolchildren, on their way home after classes, walked to the theater to see where fathers of their classmates perished. *Enterprise* newsboys were busy selling an extra edition of the paper. Isadore Osheroff sold 1,580 copies while Alex Lipsitz, who commanded a location in front of the Enterprise Building at 60 Main Street, sold 1,015 copies. The paper's circulation department had six carriers on the streets, and they sold 4,625 copies. Considered the highest-selling edition of the paper to that date, circulation manager Bert Carleton stated that sales of the edition exceeded 7,000 copies.[22]

Mayor Rowe spent the remainder of Monday personally visiting the families of every fallen firefighter and put regular city business on hold.

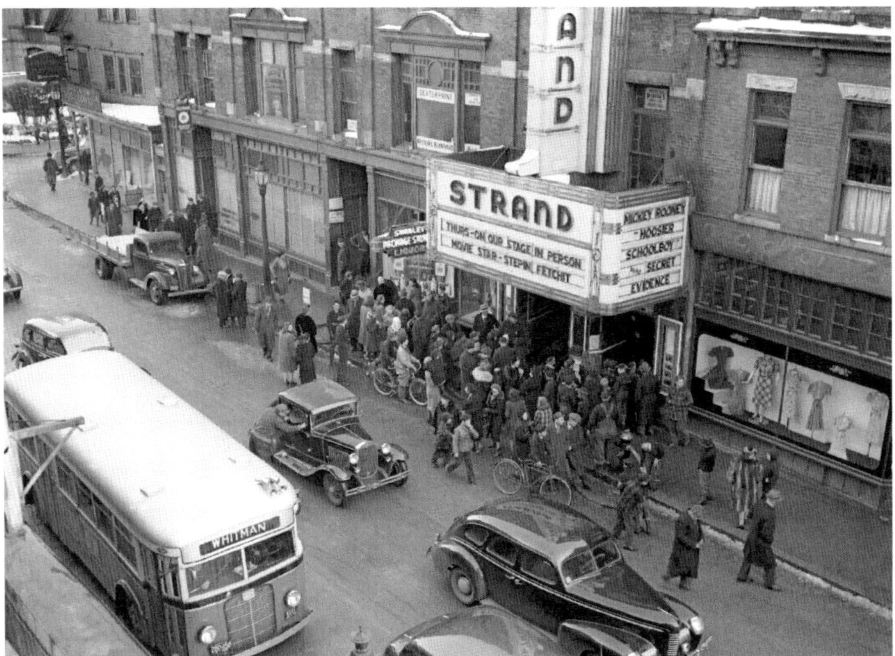

On the morning of the fire, spectators flocked to the Strand Theatre entrance on School Street, where the only evidence of the deadly blaze was the fire hose leading from the hydrant into the theater, March 10, 1941. *Bauman Collection, Stonehill College.*

Many groups and organizations canceled meetings and other activities out of respect for the dead and in shock over the enormity of the fire. Everyone's conversations revolved around the fire, both fact and fiction. The mayor ordered flags at half-mast for a period of thirty days. Central Fire Station, home of Squad A, Engine Company 1 and Ladder Company 1, was hit the hardest, having lost the most men in the fire. Ten of the thirteen fallen were from this station. After the fire, Central Fire Station was draped in black mourning cloth, also for a period of thirty days. It is assumed but not confirmed that other fire houses were also draped in mourning cloth. Mayor Rowe declared Wednesday, March 12, a citywide day of mourning. Schools and government offices would be closed. Establishments offering entertainment or selling liquor were to remain closed until 6:00 p.m. License commissioners Bowles and Tevlin were ordered by the mayor to suspend all entertainment permits for both Tuesday night and Wednesday. Restaurants could open, but they had to close their shades. The mayor asked that banks and manufacturing plants, which continued to operate, pause for a moment of silence in memory of the deceased firemen. The mayor's official proclamation read:

> *In respect to the memory of the brave firemen who heroically met death in the Strand Theatre disaster Monday, I, as mayor of Brockton, hereby proclaim Wednesday, March 12, all day as a period of mourning for the entire city. I am sure that all places of business which legally can and all places of entertainment, municipal departments and schools will comply with my order to close and remain closed until 6 P.M. as a whole-hearted community expression of tribute to the dead and sympathy to those left behind.*

Additionally, gasoline stations closed between the hours of 9:00 a.m. and 3:00 p.m., and all WPA (Works Progress Administration) projects were halted for the day.

On the morning of Tuesday, March 11, 1941, the sixty thousand–plus citizens of Brockton awoke to a city bedecked with flags at half-mast and a light snow blanketing the city in a pall of white. Chief Dickinson issued General Order No. 656, which stated: "Because of the emergency existing and because members of the deceased firemen's families have requested that their comrades act as bearers to their funerals on Wednesday morning, it will be necessary for both platoons to report for duty on Wednesday morning roll call, to be at 7:00 A.M., 'in uniform.'" The order went

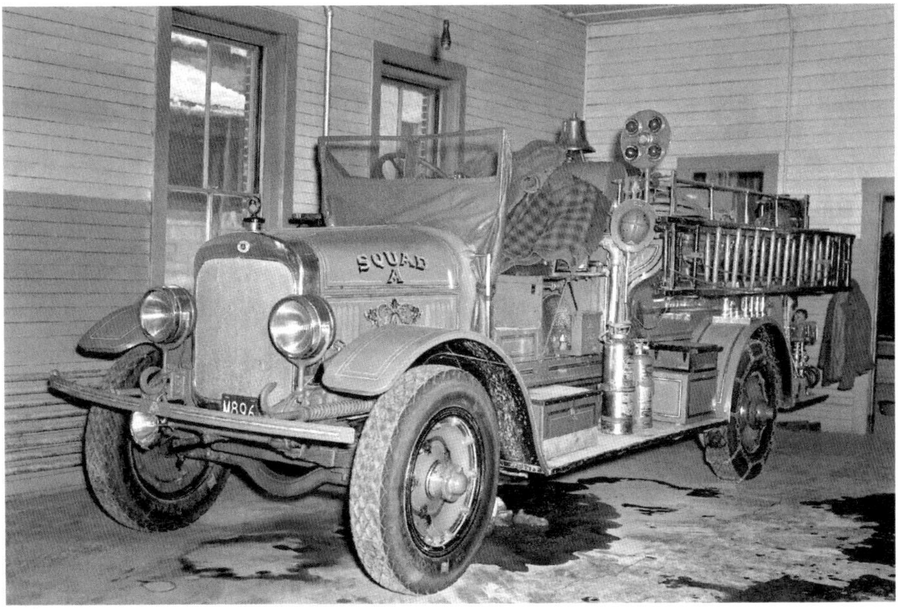

This photo shows the Squad A fire engine parked at Central Fire Station after the fire. Four members of the crew were killed and several others injured. *Bauman Collection, Stonehill College.*

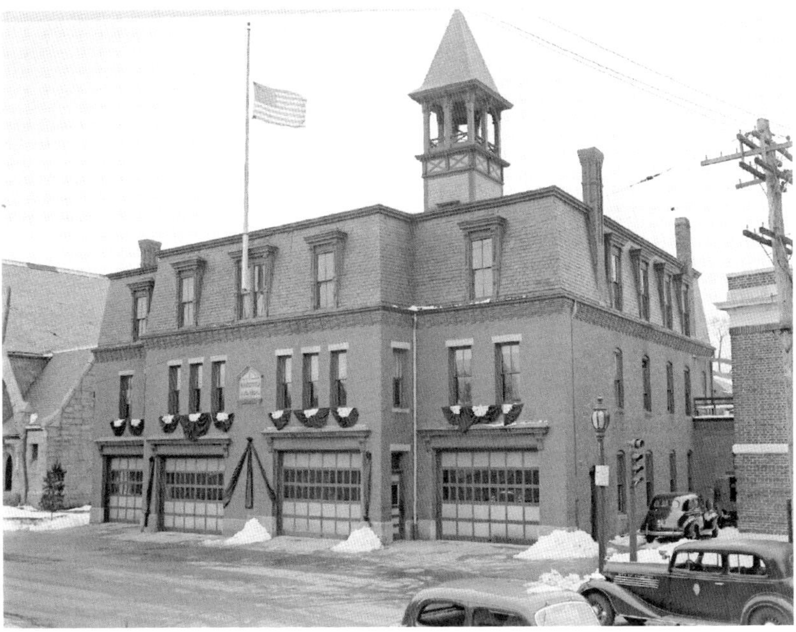

Central Fire Station, home of Squad A, Engine Company 1 and Ladder Company 1, is draped with mourning cloth after the fire. *Bauman Collection, Stonehill College.*

on to list each funeral and men chosen as bearers.[23] On the evening of Tuesday, March 11, 1941, the attention of the entire city turned to the greater toll: twelve women were now widows and twenty-four children fatherless, nineteen of these children being under the age of twenty-one and the youngest only six. Only two of the firemen had no children. With Bartholomew Herlihy still clinging to life, the wakes of his twelve brother firemen took place on Tuesday evening. Only three caskets would be open, those of Captain John Carroll, William Murphy and Matthew McGeary.

Carroll and McGeary were waked on different floors in the McGlinchy-Russell Funeral Home; Lieutenant Raymond A. Mitchell, Martin Lipper and Frederick Kelley were waked at the Hickey Funeral Home. Lipper and Kelley were waked in adjoining rooms on the first floor while Mitchell was on the second floor. Good friends, John Malcolm McNeill and Henry Sullivan were waked together at the Conley Funeral Home. Roy McKeraghan and George Collins were waked at Sampson's Funeral Home. Denis Murphy, William O'Brien and William Murphy were waked in their respective homes. Wives and children were weary not only from the strain and stress of death but also from greeting thousands of mourners. An unknown attendee of the wakes remarked to the *Enterprise*: "I guess everyone in town has gone to a wake." Fellow firefighters joined the lines of mourners, as did Deputy Chiefs Lynch and Murphy and Chief Dickinson.

Ten of the fallen, all but Daniel O'Brien and Roy McKeraghan, would be laid to rest on Wednesday, March 12, 1941; their last alarm would be sounded on Thursday. Unable to attend any of the funerals, Deputy Chief Lynch and Fire Chief Dickinson paid a silent tribute to their departed comrades by placing a wreath on Squad A at the Central Fire Station. They had previously visited the home of each departed fireman and also those still in the hospital. Five of the fallen would be buried with full military honors, attesting to their wartime service in the First World War. Those who served their country as well as their city were Daniel O'Brien, Henry Sullivan, Martin Lipper, Frederick Kelley and John Malcolm O'Neill.

As their comrades were laid to rest, nine firemen remained in the Brockton Hospital. Rumors and reports around the city proclaimed that Bartholomew Herlihy had died. On Wednesday morning, those rumors proved to be false, but his condition had worsened. The other men slowly recovered from their injuries. Arthur Hammerquist was burned, as was Lieutenant Ernest McRae, William Kelleher and Jeremiah Sheehan. Lieutenant John Buckley and John Cashman suffered leg injuries, and William McGowan was recovering from general injuries and Courtney Simpson, back injuries. Sadly, at 7:44 p.m. on

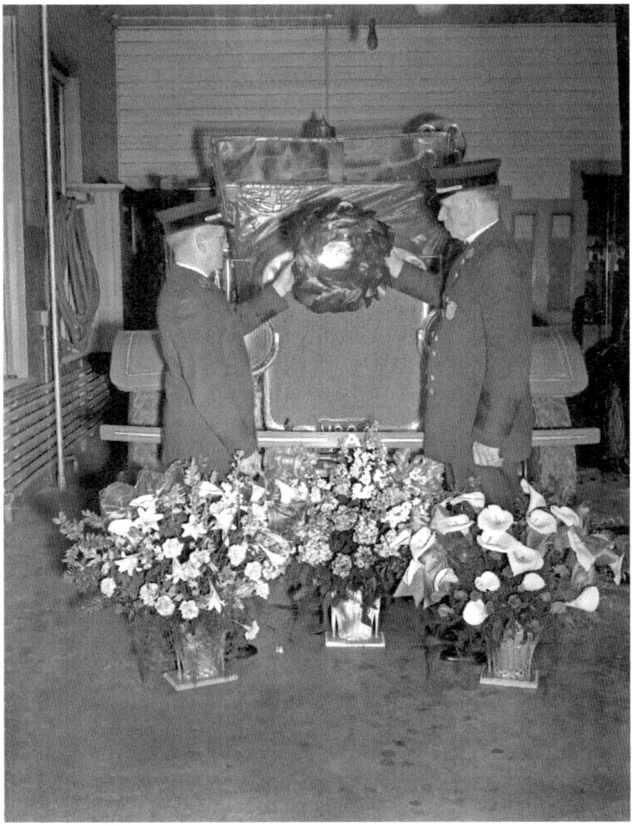

Deputy Chief Lawrence F. Lynch and Fire Chief Frank F. Dickinson, who were unable to attend funerals of those killed, pay silent tribute to their departed comrades by placing a wreath on Squad A's engine, March 12, 1941. *Bauman Collection, Stonehill College.*

Wednesday, March 12, forty-five-year-old Bartholomew Herlihy succumbed to his injuries and became the fire's thirteenth victim. Of those men pulled alive from the rubble, Herlihy was the most severely injured. Hit by timber, bricks and steel, he died without regaining consciousness. Herlihy spent his twenty-one years with the fire department assigned to Ladder Company 1 out of the city's Central Fire Station.

Herlihy, like five of his fellow deceased firefighters, was a veteran of World War I and was buried from St. Patrick's Roman Catholic Church with full military honors. Attending the funeral were thirteen of his friends from D Company, 101st Infantry, AEF (American Expeditionary Force), Herlihy's unit in the war. Held on Saturday, Herlihy's funeral Mass was said by Father Joseph Kenney, assisted by Father Morrisroe. Fred Hendrick, who had opened his office in the Washburn Building as a refuge for tired and injured firemen, sang "Pie Jesu" and "Miseremini Mei" before a church filled with mourners that included Mayor Rowe and state representatives Joseph Downey and Charles McCaffrey.[24]

Even as the trucks began to return to stations minus many of their crews, messages of sympathy and offers of help began to stream in from all corners of the country. So many telegrams arrived that a full-time courier was needed to deliver them to Mayor Rowe and Chief Dickinson. Among the messages received by Chief Dickinson was a letter from Frank Heron of the Burlington, Vermont Fire Fighters Association, the chief's hometown, which read in part, "Members of the association wish to extend to you and members of your department our heartfelt sympathy and also ask that you convey our condolences to families of the unfortunate firemen who lost their lives in the service of humanity." Letters were received from the New York City fire commissioner John McElligot, Commissioner M.J. Corrigan of Chicago and a score of other leaders of departments large and small. From the volunteer Quinsnicket Fire Department in Lincoln, Rhode Island, came these words: "Your department has maintained the true tradition of firemen and their unselfish devotion to the safety of others. Our hats are off to the Brockton Fire Department."

The San Francisco Fire Department messaged the chief: "Our heartfelt sympathy and condolences to your department and to the bereaved families of your comrades who gave their lives in behalf of the fire service." From Palm Beach, Florida, came a telegram from Charles McCarthy, whose father, Captain Charles McCarthy, was assigned to Station 2 in Campello. The younger McCarthy wrote, "My heart goes out to you on your great loss. It's a great shock to me and I know it is to you. God was watching over many of the boys, including my dad, and I am grateful. My prayers for those still alive. With deepest sympathy to you and the men under you."[25]

Offers of help were received from two of the larger fire departments in the area. Thomas Skudder Burgin, mayor of Quincy, Massachusetts, sent these words: "Just ask and if we have it, you'll get it." In addition, he sent the Quincy fire chief to Brockton to offer direct aid. Fire Chief Samuel Pope of the Boston Fire Department called Chief Dickinson to offer, "Anything the Boston Fire Department has in way of men and equipment is at the command of Brockton."[26]

Alton Hall "Blackie" Blackington, a noted photojournalist with the *Boston Herald* and a close friend of Dickinson, wrote, "My heart goes out to you and all members of your department. Many people will remember the fire scenes I have flashed upon a thousand screens in the past twenty-five years and how many times I have said 'A man can die but once. He is just as much a hero if he is killed at a fire as if he were shot down in a plane or died going over the top.'"

Mayor Rowe received a telegram from Brockton native and Texas oil tycoon Edgar Davis with these words of support: "My heart goes out in deepest sympathy in the terrible catastrophe in the city of Brockton and the fire department has sustained and particularly to the families of those who died or were injured in their faithful and courageous performance of their duty."

A week after the Strand fire, the Plymouth County Fire Chief's Club held its regularly scheduled dinner meeting in Brockton. Those who were chosen to speak at this meeting had been at the Strand. Chief Dickinson presided over the meeting and opened it with a moment of silence in memory of the deceased firemen. Several chiefs spoke, as did Mayor Rowe. Dickinson was the final speaker and, as quoted in the *Brockton Enterprise*, spoke these words: "I'm not going to say much as I don't feel like talking. But I do want to say that when a man has his troubles he finds out his friends. I found many I didn't even know I had. And to all of them, chiefs and others, I want to express my sincere thanks for being real friends." In response to the flood of mail and telegrams, Chief Dickinson responded, "It takes something like this to make you realize how many fine people there are."[27]

Dickinson was by all accounts a good chief and a good firefighter. Appointed to the Brockton Fire Department on June 17, 1891, he was appointed chief of the department in 1928. Following the Strand disaster, a short piece was printed in tribute to the chief in a news article that is today unattributed but speaks highly of Dickinson, the man:

> *Tall men who bend to the storm and don't break, even as the rugged buckwheat of the field were noticeable last week…in especial, one tall and gray man who put his responsibilities above his grief. Department short 35 men one night, city to be protected, his the job, he went about his work as if he were a man of steel…emotions battered down, brain clicking, voice firm, eyes dry, he did what he had to do without a sign. "I suppose you feel it the same as everyone else" it was suggested…"down to the tips of my shoes, mister, and it's why I'm not going to show it" was the tense reply. The tall man was Fire Chief Dickinson, who has bent and never broken through many storms…one of them the week before, when he buried the woman with whom he had walked through the years.*

This tribute to Dickinson was the only mention throughout the days following the catastrophe on School Street that of the fact that the chief's wife had died barely two weeks before the fire.

In the weeks that followed the fire, Mayor Rowe would highly recommend Father Lawrence Morrisroe to be a recipient of the Carnegie Medal of Honor. The mayor's letter to the medal commission read:

> *May I recommend for your consideration recognition from your commission of Rev. Lawrence P. Morrisroe, curate at St. Patrick's church at Brockton, Mass. During the memorable Strand Theatre fire on Monday, March 10, 1941 he performed feats of unusual heroism by entering the building to give consolation and absolution to many firemen pinned under wreckage. The risks that he took and the places in the burning building where he went were the same as those of the firemen themselves and were in the immediate vicinity of the exact spot of the disaster. While he was giving consolation and absolution to the dead and dying he was in the imminent danger of further collapse of the roof which had fallen at that time from the balcony....Fr. Morrisroe's activity that morning showed a bona fide exhibition of supreme bravery and entire disregard for personal safety.*

As passionate as was the mayor's plea for recognition, Morrisroe was passed over for the coveted recognition.[28]

In the aftermath of the Strand fire, an interesting letter was published in a newspaper for which only the news clipping survives. The letter is headlined "Bravery of Firemen" and states:

> *I wonder whether or not Mayor Kane of Woburn is a regular reader of our Boston papers. If so I'd like to know if he had changed his opinion of the "glamor boys" as he so maliciously nicknamed all members of the State Firemen's Ass'n last week at the State House when over 100 firemen were ejected from our government seat. I don't know what Mr. Kane has against the uniformed men of this State, but for the last few years I've read often of the outrages he has perpetrated against the firemen of his hometown....He should read carefully the full account of the tragedy at Brockton Monday morning when 12 brave and courageous men sacrificed their lives, and scores of others were injured in the performance of their duties. I feel sure that the brave men who died in Brockton will not be forgotten for a long time to come. It was certainly one of the most tragic happenings I have heard of in my 32 years. Mr. Kane should absorb deeply into his mind and heart the story told by Rev. Fr. Morrisroe who fought his way into the blaze to administer the last rites of the Catholic Church to men who were veritably buried alive. Maybe it would change his opinion of these glamor*

> *boys. I have the greatest respect for all firemen and hope someday, providing I'm the man that those who died were, to become a member of the Boston fire department.* [signed] *YOUNG ASPIRANT TO THE BOSTON FIRE DEPARTMENT.*

Another letter from the same paper was signed Fireman's Daughter, headlined "Fireman" and read:

> *Perhaps Mayor Kane of Woburn, if you have read the papers you know of the tragedy that has troubled Brockton. Mayor Rowe can tell you only too well that the firemen do more than knit and sleep. When the gong sounds for a fireman he never knows if it is to be his last alarm. Not only in Brockton but the whole countryside will mourn for those unsung heroes. Before you blow off steam again, mayor Kane, why don't you think?*

Certainly the Strand sparked emotions as only severe tragedy can do.[29]

Inquest

Barely had the fire been extinguished than talk turned to its cause. From all accounts, the fire was believed to have started in the basement under the candy counter, and when Captain Stack and his men arrived, they deployed the cellar pipes to extinguish the blaze. A photo taken of firefighters cleaning up the basement after the fire shows severe charring at the ceiling but little damage at the cellar floor. In fact, one could still read labels on boxes. However, the fire had spread through the wall to the roof, possibly through the building's ventilation system, where it burned until it broke through and the roof gave way, trapping and killing the thirteen firefighters. Speculation also surrounds the actual roof collapse. One headline in the *Brockton Enterprise* speculated that a film explosion may have weakened the roof, although no evidence was found to support this. A more common theory reported by several newspapers was that heavy snow on the roof contributed to the collapse. However, a photo of the theater roof taken by photographer Stanley Bauman two days after the fire shows little snow on the roof of the theater or on the roofs of nearby buildings.

Herbert Ferris of the Electrical Trades Local, who assisted with the rescue of the trapped firefighters, told the *Brockton Enterprise* on March 10, 1941:

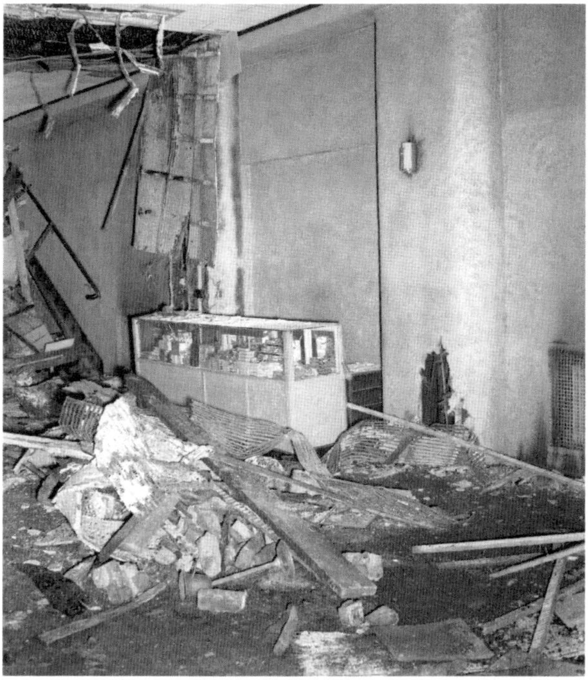

The fire is believed to have started in basement directly below this candy counter, March 13, 1941. *Bauman Collection, Stonehill College.*

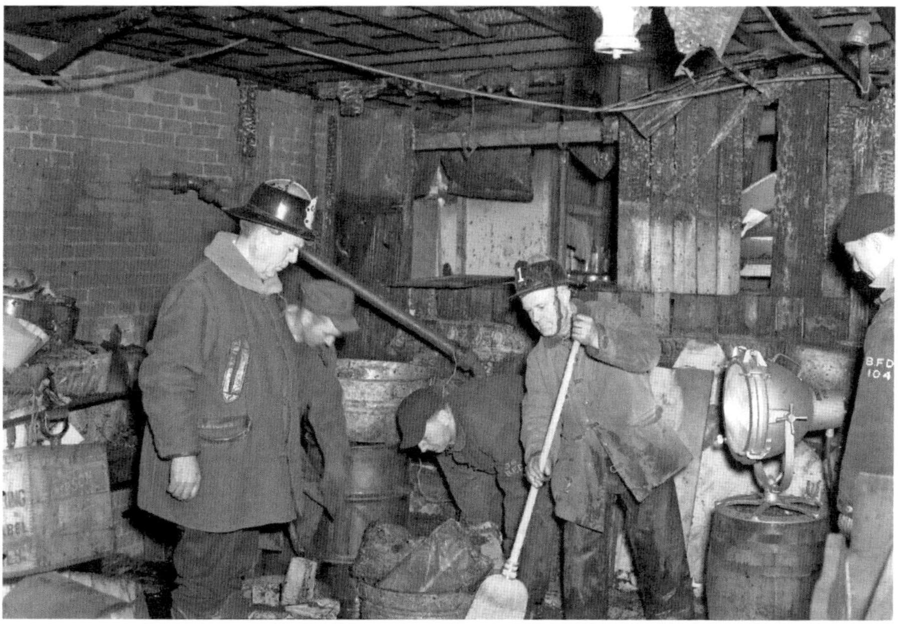

Firefighters clean up the basement of the Strand Theatre, where the fire is believed to have originated. *Bauman Collection, Stonehill College.*

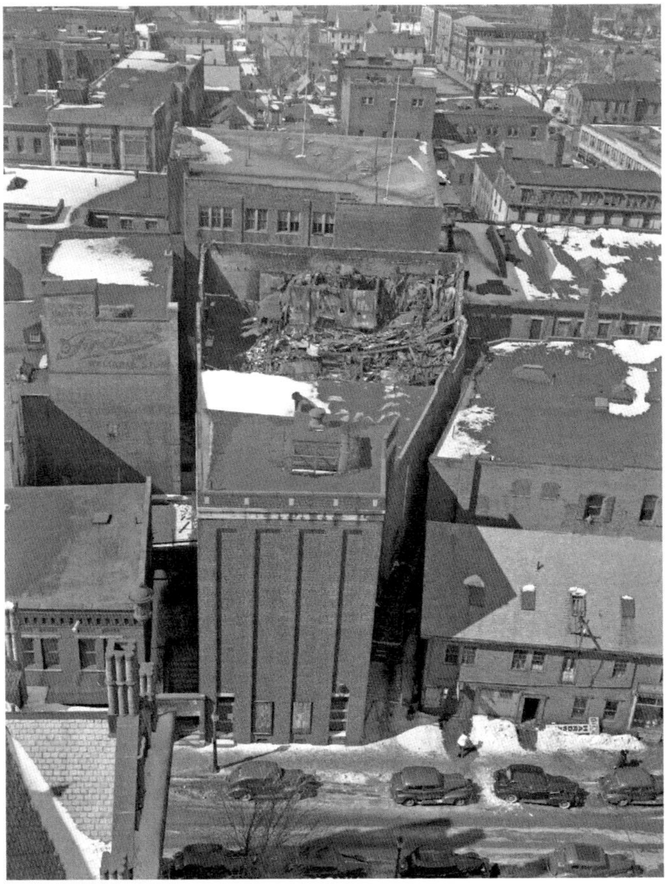

The view from Brockton City Hall of the Strand Theatre shows the collapsed roof and how the proximity of the surrounding buildings made access difficult, March 13, 1941. *Bauman Collection, Stonehill College.*

> *To one familiar with construction, the cause of the tragedy goes back to the days when the building was built.... When it was built no metal beds were set in to hold a steel girder which held up the roof over the balcony. The fire worked up into a corner beam which had supported the girder and the flames heated the metal red hot. When water struck the red hot metal, it buckled and let down the roof.*

A formal inquest was set up to answer these questions. Scheduled for Wednesday, March 12, 1941, the same day as ten of the funerals, the confidential inquest was conducted by state fire marshal Stephen J. Garrity; Edward H. Murtagh, the state's assistant fire marshal; inspector John Shaw; Lieutenant Albert L. Brouilard of the Massachusetts State Police; and state trooper George Grady, on assignment with the fire

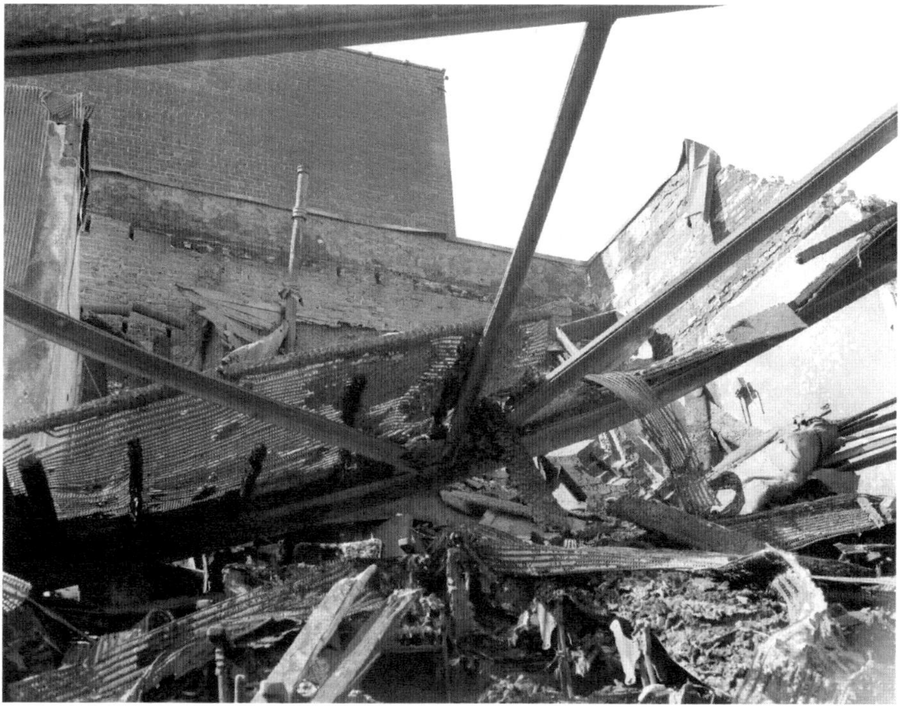

This view of the collapsed roof shows the beams that buckled in the fire and that are believed to have broken free from the walls, causing the Strand Theatre's roof to collapse. *Bauman Collection, Stonehill College.*

marshal's office. Brouilard was assigned to the case by Edmund R. Dewing, the district attorney, and charged with investigating the possibility of criminal liability. Held behind closed doors in Chief Dickinson's office at the Central Fire Station, the inquest was only open to witnesses. Among the witnesses called to give testimony before the inquest were Frank Clements, manager of the Strand; stagehand Andrew Butler; custodian and the person who first saw the fire, Christopher Moore; his assistant, Roger Thunert, who pulled the alarm at Fire Alarm Box 1311; motion picture operator Ray Shattuck; stagehand Israel Baker; Officer Sanford K. Alger; William Fencer, property manager; Dorothy Chubbuck, relief cashier; and candy counter attendant Tanya Waschuck. Only members of the inquest and witnesses were allowed entry to Chief Dickinson's office, where the questioning was taking place. News reporters, as well as Frederick Lieberman of Proven Pictures and lessee of the Strand, were denied entrance.

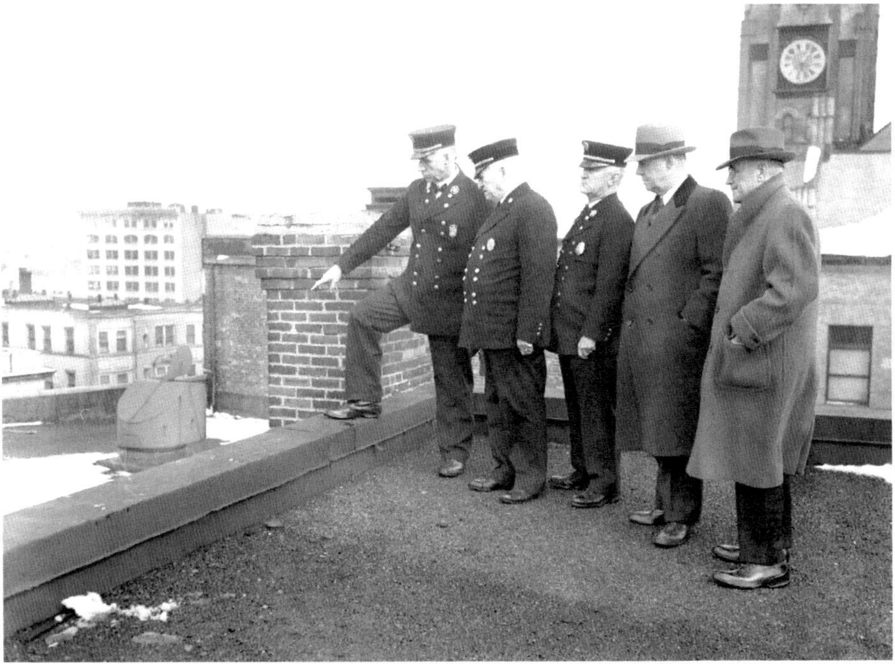

From one of the adjacent building's roofs, Chief Frank F. Dickinson points out roof collapse damage. With him *(from left to right)* are Chief David Teirney, Arlington; Chief Seldon Allen, Brookline; Brockton building superintendent William Green; and state fire marshal Stephen Garrity. *Bauman Collection, Stonehill College.*

No indication of what was said at the inquiry was given by Garrity. He would only tell reporters that when he had finished his inquest, the evidence would be studied, but findings would not be released before the following Monday. He then reportedly left for Indianapolis the following day, Thursday, March 13, 1941. Assistant state fire marshal Edward H. Murtagh was not as closemouthed about his opinions on the fire's origin, telling a reporter outside Central Fire Station, "In my opinion the Strand Theatre Fire was incendiary." This caused the *Enterprise* to run headlines "Strand Theatre Fire Set, Says Murtagh" and "Tells *Enterprise* Firebug at Work." Murtagh gave a more in-depth interview with the *Boston Globe* the day before the inquest, and his opinion was reported: "After spending several hours in the 'examination of the gutted structure he had removed every chance of it being a natural fire.' The wiring was perfect and the place in the basement where the fire started would not normally be subjected to excessive heat." In addition, Murtagh told the *Globe*, "There were several rubbish barrels in the basement but there was no evidence of fire in or about them." He also found that the basement did not have old films stored in it that might have "burned fiercely enough to give the fire its early impetus." Murtagh went on to say that he

> *had determined the fire started in the flooring above an air conductor. The beams and other woodwork at this point were completely eaten away…and "It would not have been difficult for someone to place something on top of the air conductor and walk away without being detected." The flames then climbed between the walls to the main floor and balcony and broke near the roof where his "minute examination of the balcony where the roof collapsed"…convinced him that a number of the steel girders supporting the roof had buckled under the intense heat.*[30]

Lending credence to Murtagh's statements was the questioning of a seventeen-year-old boy who was in the city during the fire and was heard discussing details of the fire in Portland, Maine. Notified of this young

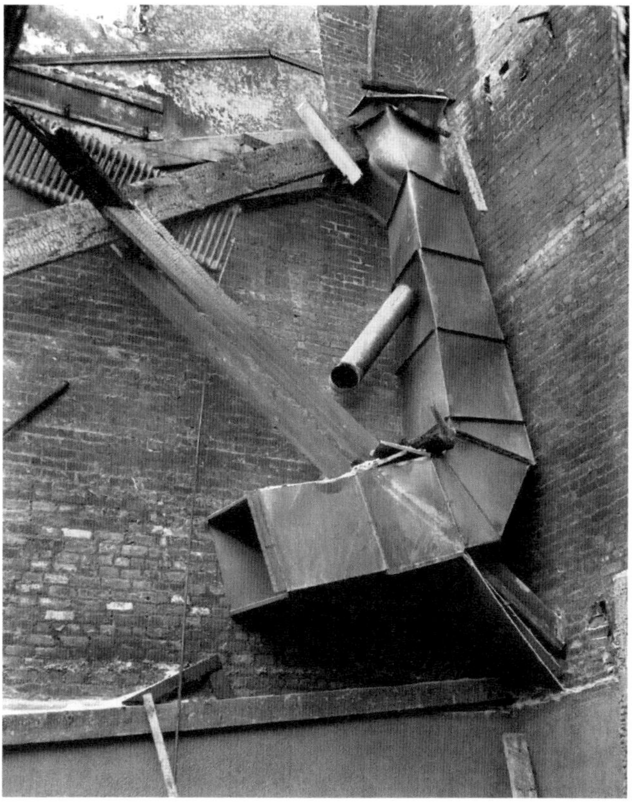

One theory of the fire was that it spread through the walls and ventilation system of the theater. Taken three days after the fire, on March 13, 1941, this photo shows one of the theater's large ventilation shafts. *Bauman Collection, Stonehill College.*

man being a person of interest, Portland and Brockton police questioned him for several hours, but he was eventually eliminated as a suspect. In response to questions about Murtagh's statements, Garrity would only say, "I have not completed my investigation, therefore I cannot say if it was incendiary or not."

When the findings were released in April, the *Enterprise* headline read, "Cause Unknown in Strand Fire." The *Brockton Enterprise* would publish the full report as follows:

> *At an inquest held by me at the Brockton fire department on Wednesday, March 12 inquiry was made into the facts and circumstances connected with a fire which occurred on March 10 at the Strand Theatre on School Street, Brockton. A large number of witnesses, 22 in all, were called and an exhaustive inquiry was conducted in an effort to ascertain the cause of the fire. A thorough investigation has been made of all the information developed at the inquest and the evidence has been considered for its value in determining the cause of the fire. No evidence of incendiarism was found and no facts developed which indicate the origin from a specific accidental cause. The cause of the fire will therefore be recorded in the department files as of unknown origin.*[31]

A copy of the report was forwarded, along with transcripts of evidence taken at the inquest, to district attorney Edmund R. Dewing, but no conclusion was ever made on what caused one of the deadliest fires in the city's history.

4

The Fallen

As the sun set on March 10, 1941, Brockton residents mourned the loss of twelve firefighters. Over twenty additional men were recovering from injuries, either at the Brockton Hospital or at home. Still others continued to work despite injuries. The most seriously injured was Bartholomew Herlihy of Ladder Company 1. When Herlihy was brought from the wreckage, a doctor present at the scene declared, "His back is surely broken."[32] The *Brockton Daily Enterprise* listed his condition as "probably will die—spine and other injuries."[33] Bartholomew Herlihy would succumb to his injuries two days later, the thirteenth firefighter to die.

Firefighters admitted to the Brockton Hospital with serious injuries included:

- John H. Cashman, Squad A, leg injury
- Arthur Hammerquist, Engine 4, burns to hands, knees and face
- Melvin McRae, Engine 4, exhaustion
- William E. Kelleher, Engine 1, burns to face and hands
- Jeremiah Sheehan, burns to hands and feet
- Lieutenant John Buckley, Squad A, leg injury
- Lieutenant Ernest McRae, burns to hands, face and feet
- William Hogan, back injuries and shock
- Courtney Simpson, Engine 5, back injury[34]

Those treated at the Brockton Hospital and released to recover at home or treated and released at the scene included:

- Andrew Johnson, Ladder 3
- George E. Maloney, Ladder 3
- John Dowd, Engine 1
- Lieutenant Thomas Barren, Engine 1
- Walter Langley
- Deputy John Murphy
- Thomas B. Monahan, back injury
- William Lipper
- Fred Peck
- James McGeary
- Captain Herbert Gullefer
- Lieutenant Patrick Long
- Captain Patrick Stack, injured hand
- Lieutenant William H. Bussey
- Gregory Noonan
- Frank Carrier
- James F. Toomey, exposure[35]

Four days after the fire, on March 14, 1941, in addition to those who died, sixteen were unable to report to duty. However, according to the *Brockton Enterprise*, many worked despite their injuries and against doctors' orders, including:

- Walter McLaren, strapped back
- William Hogan, strapped back
- Lawrence Johnson, injured back and shoulders
- Lieutenant Frederick Papineau, crushed toe
- Cornelius Burke (injury not listed)
- John Kelley (injury not listed)
- Captain Charles McCarthy of Campello, back and right hip injuries
- Eric Nordeen, nervous exhaustion
- Oswald W. Kuplast, strapped back
- Frank Cameron, strapped back[36]

On Tuesday, March 11, 1941, the *Brockton Enterprise* reported the number of men missing at each of Brockton's six fire stations from death or injuries. Central Fire Station (Station 1), located at 42 Pleasant Street, lost twenty men, thirteen from first platoon and seven from second. Station 2, located at 945 Main Street in the Campello section of the city, lost one man from first platoon but no one from second platoon. Station 3, located at 916 North Main Street, lost one man from second platoon but no one from first platoon. Station 4 located at the corner of Crescent and Lyman Streets, lost two men from first platoon and two men from second platoon. Station 5, known as the Battles Street Station, lost six men from first platoon but no one from second platoon. Station 6, located at the corner of Belmont and Boylston Streets, lost two men from first platoon and one man from second platoon. Death and injuries hit the Battles Street and Central Stations hardest. The crews of both of these stations were assigned twenty-four-hour duty, and volunteer substitutes helped bolster Central Fire Station's depleted crew. Among the substitutes were Wallace Campbell, Kenneth White, Michael Principe, Edward Martin Francis Dupuis and P. Clark Murphy. Murphy, who had been appointed to the department in 1911, had retired two years earlier in 1939 but returned to duty to fill in while the injured recovered.[37]

In total, over thirty-five men were injured. Most were able to return to work within a few days or weeks, but for some, the journey was much longer. The list of injured, however, is not complete. *Brockton Enterprise* accounts of the injured list some men but not others, and the paper did little follow-up on the injured after the fire, with a few exceptions. One article from March 10, 1943, on the second anniversary of the fire, gives an account of twenty-three injured firefighters. However, the list includes the names of Harold L. Weeks, Harold Shurtleff and James McAulliffe, who were not noted as injured in the 1941 newspaper articles. Others listed as injured in 1941 news accounts, including Captain Patrick Stack, Lieutenant William H. Bussey and Captain Herbert Gullefer, were omitted from the 1943 article. For Lieutenant Bussey, his injury marked the seventy-third time he had been injured in the line of duty during his twenty-nine-year career with the Brockton Fire Department. Off duty since January 1941 due to injuries sustained at a Stacy-Adams Shoe Factory fire in the city, he answered the call of the second alarm and worked until midmorning before being sent home after being treated for burns to his head and body. City directories list him as retired within a few years of the fire.

Captain Charles G. McCarthy, of Engine Company 2, Campello Station, fell twice during the Strand Theatre fire, injuring his hip. The first time, he slipped while working on the stage, and later, he tripped over a seat edge after losing his footing in loose plaster while working in the balcony. On Monday, March 24, 1941, two weeks after the fire, the *Brockton Enterprise* reported that the captain's hip injury, which had continued to bother him since the fire, had been X-rayed at the Brockton Hospital. He had stayed on duty knowing that the department was short-handed. However, after the X-ray, the injured hip was "strapped-up," and he was ordered home to rest until at least Thursday, when he would be examined again. This was not the first time McCarthy had been injured in the line of duty. During his thirty-five-year career, he had been hospitalized for a fractured skull, injured ribs and various other injuries.

John Buckley, the commander of Squad A the day of the fire who was rescued from debris in the back corner of the theater, spent three weeks in the hospital recovering from a leg injury. Eventually, Lieutenant Buckley returned to work and rose through the ranks; he was promoted to captain in 1944 and deputy chief in 1949. He retired from the department in 1957 at the age of sixty-five. William Lipper recovered from his injures but could no longer work the ladder. When Lipper finally returned to work, he became the chief's driver, a position he held until his retirement in 1971.[38] William J. McGowan was not reported on injury lists in the 1941 *Enterprise* articles. Yet on March 22, 1941, a *Daily Boston Globe* article titled "Another Brockton Theatre Fireman Is Near Death" reported that McGowan was released from the hospital on March 13 after being treated for burns but on March 21 returned to the Brockton Hospital, where he was hovering between life and death after a relapse stemming from severe hemorrhages.[39] In 1943, the *Enterprise* noted that he spent a total of eight weeks in the hospital for burns and internal bleeding. McGowan recovered from his injuries, returned to the department and retired from his career as a firefighter in the 1950s. Arthur Hammerquist spent three weeks in the hospital recovering from burns but would also return to work. John H. Cashman suffered back and leg injuries and was hospitalized while recovering from surgery to have cartilage removed from his knee.

Two firefighters were pensioned after the fire. William E. Kelleher, who had a dramatic rescue after the collapse from the rafters of the theater, and William H. Berry would not return to work. The exact reason for being pensioned was not noted in 1943, but initial reports in 1941 listed Kelleher's injuries as a concussion and burns to his face and hands and Berry's as burns and cuts, for which he was treated at the police station but not hospitalized.

Several firefighters faced months and even years of recovery before being able to return to work. Cornelius J. Burke was out of work for six months due to a severely injured back. Thomas B. Monaghan was out of work for nearly two years suffering from back, arm and torso injuries. Alice LaLiberte recalled in an interview that she had been dating Monaghan's son Robert in 1941. Prior to Robert's being drafted in 1942, Monaghan's wife tried,

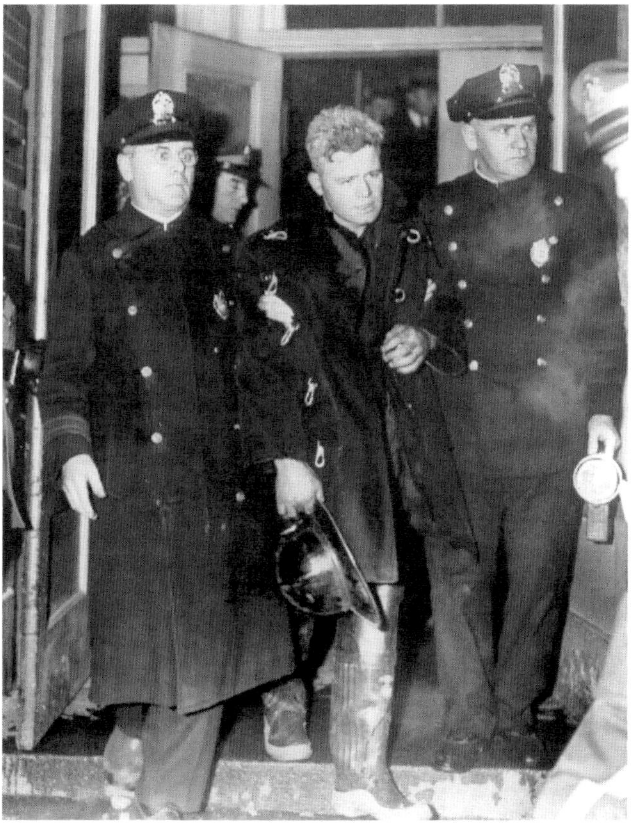

Firefighter Melvin J. McRae, Engine Co. 4, brother of Lieutenant Ernest McRae, is assisted from the theater suffering from exhaustion after the collapse. *Brockton Fire Museum.*

unsuccessfully, to keep her son out of the draft by citing the need for him to help support the family. According to city directories, Monaghan would eventually return to his job as a ladderman until his retirement in the early 1950s. George E. Maloney was also out of work for almost two years recovering from back injuries. An article about the first anniversary memorial noted that Maloney attended the ceremony but wore a brace as he continued recovering from back surgery. Lieutenant Ernest McRae suffered one of the most severe injuries. Out of work for about eighteen months, he returned to the department assigned to office duty. The rubber gloves McRae wore while fighting the fire melted to his hands in the collapse. Lieutenant McRae was transferred to a Boston hospital where plastic surgeons removed the melted rubber and began the slow process of rebuilding his hands. In 1943, it was reported that Lieutenant McRae most likely would need at least one more surgery. In all, he had ten operations, the most extensive of which included skin grafts from different parts of

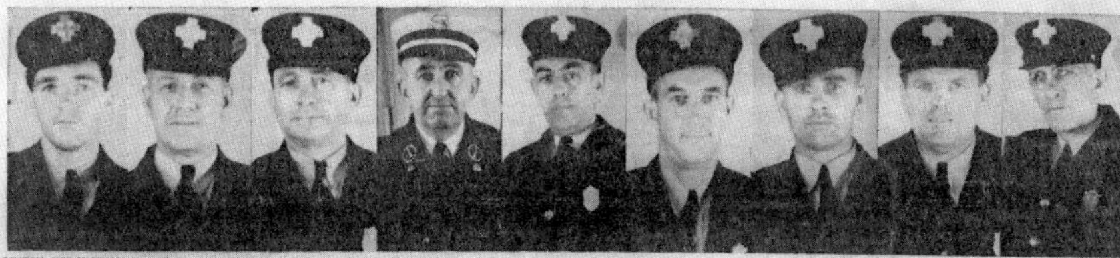

BROCKTON FIRE VICTIMS—Eight of the 13 Brockton firemen who were killed and one who was critically injured today when they were trapped in the blazing interior of the Strand Theater when the roof caved in. Left to right: William J. Murphy, Henry E. Sullivan, Dennis Murphy, Capt. John F. Carroll and Martin E. Lipper, who were killed; Bartholomew Herlihy, who was critically injured, and Malcolm McNeil, Fred F. Kelley and Daniel C. O'Brien, who were killed.

13 BROCKTON FIREMEN KILLED IN FIRE

This is one of the few news headlines announcing the death of the thirteen firefighters. The date and publication are unknown, but it is believed to be from an edition that did not publish daily, and therefore, its first publication would have been after the death of firefighter Bartholomew Herlihy on March 12, 1941. *Brockton Fire Museum.*

his body to his hands and face. Despite being permanently disabled after losing the mobility of all the fingers on one hand, McRae served in the department for an additional twenty years. McRae's injuries would lead the Brockton Fire Department to ban the use of rubber gloves by firefighters during firefighting operations, a rule still in effect today.

Yet all those who worked the fire bore the scars of that night, both visible and invisible. They survived when thirteen of their brothers had not. Those who fell were to be remembered. Per the families' request, separate funerals were held for each of the fallen thirteen.

CAPTAIN JOHN F. CARROLL

John F. Carroll was born in Brockton on February 10, 1885. Before being appointed to the Brockton Fire Department on May 10, 1909, he worked at the George E. Keith Shoe Company. He was assigned to Engine 4 on December 20, 1909, as a driver of the hose wagon (when horses were still being used). Carroll was appointed lieutenant on December 19, 1921, remaining with Engine 4 until November 18, 1939, when he

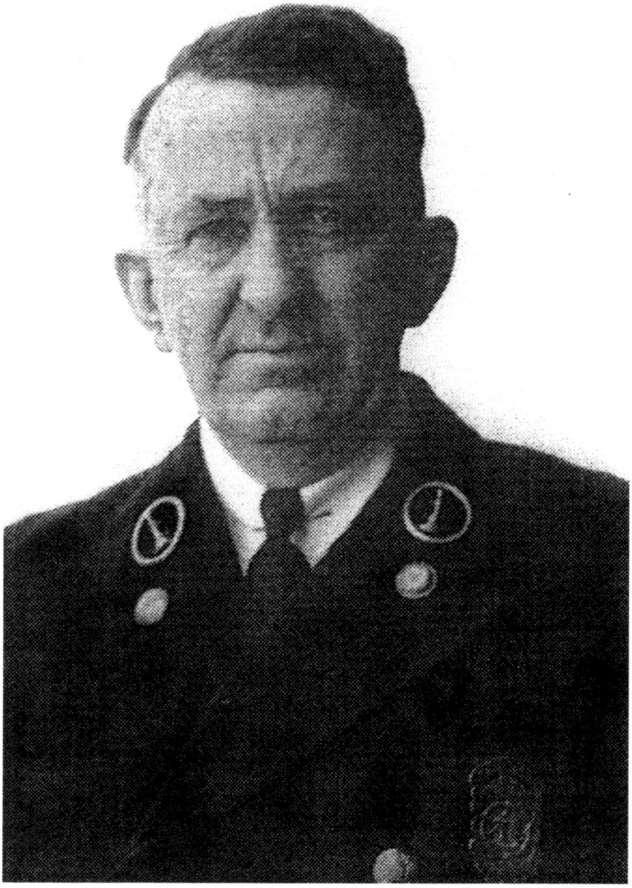

Captain John F. Carroll, fifty-seven, Ladder Company 3. *Brockton Fire Museum.*

was promoted to the rank of captain and transferred to Ladder 3 at the Battles Street Station.

Loved for his genial disposition and admired for his fine record, Carroll was not on duty the day of the Strand Theatre fire. He was called to duty when the second alarm was sounded and killed instantly in the second collapse. His body was the first found in the wreckage.

Captain Carroll married Gertrude May Coopy in 1912. The couple lived at 118 Lyman Street and had three children: John Thomas (born August 6, 1920), Marie Virginia (born 1922) and David William (born February 19, 1930). A former roller polo player (where polo was played wearing roller skates), Captain Carroll was also a regular communicant at St. Coleman's Church and a member of St. Thomas Court, Massachusetts Catholic Order of Foresters.

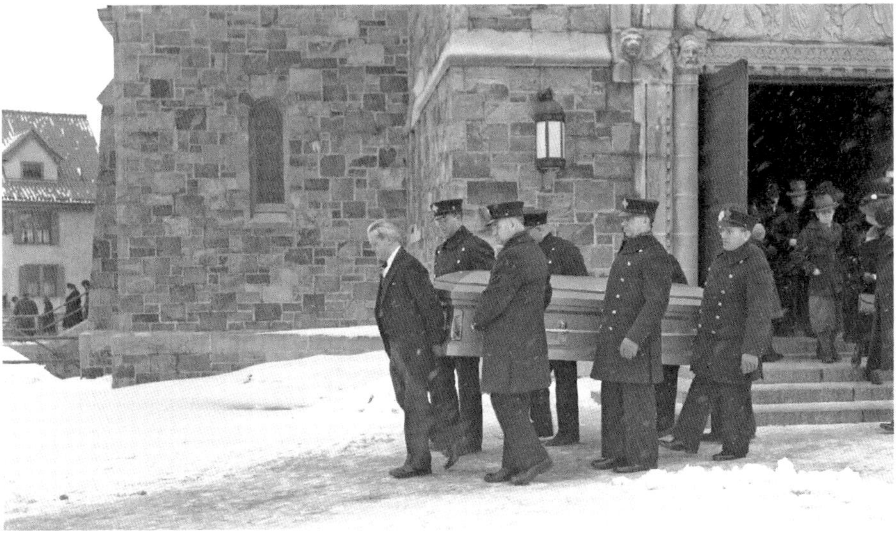

The funeral of Captain Carroll, March 12, 1941. *Bauman Collection, Stonehill College.*

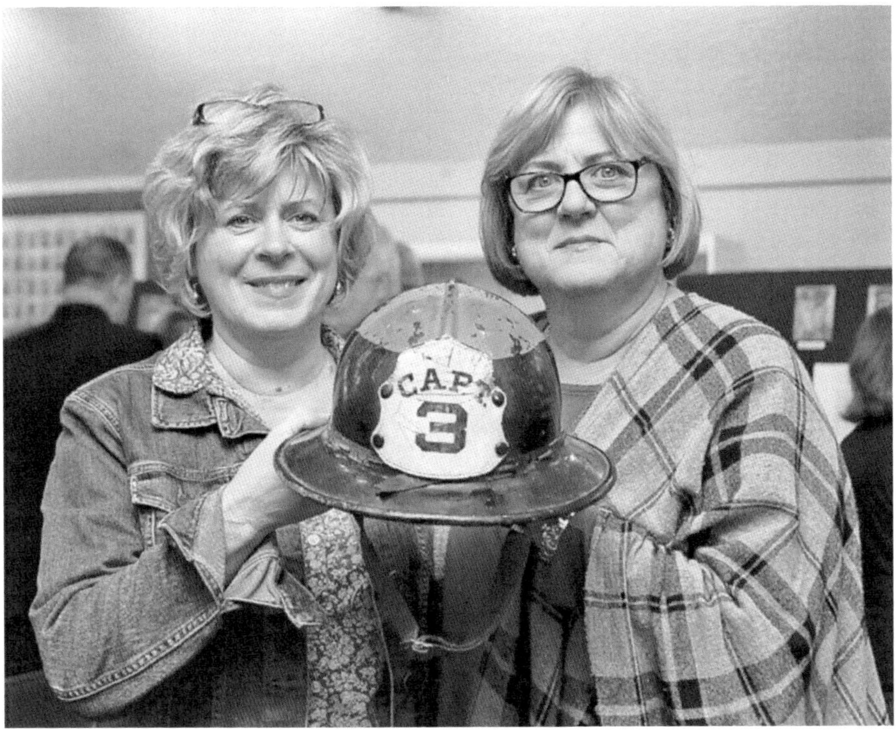

Sara Carroll (*left*) and Patricia Cruise (*right*) hold the helmet of their grandfather Captain John F. Carroll at a gathering for the families of the fallen firefighters on the eve of the seventy-fifth anniversary, March 9, 2016. *Bob Myers, 105 Fire Photos.*

Captain Carroll's wake was held at the McGlinchy-Russell Funeral Home on Main Street. A High Mass of Requiem was celebrated at St. Coleman's Church. The funeral began thirty minutes late due to traffic from the funeral procession of William J. Murphy's funeral, held at 9:00 a.m. Mass was celebrated by Reverend Edward B. Callahan with Reverend Robert Shea of Our Lady of Lourdes Church seated in the sanctuary. Bearers for Captain Carroll included fellow firemen William J. Haverty, Jeremiah J. Burke, William Stack, James C. Thomas, Richard Barry and P. Clark McCarthy, a pensioned member. Interment was in St. Michael's Cemetery in Avon, Massachusetts.

Gertrude would receive a $1,000 annuity until her death in 1950, and David would receive a $200 annuity until his eighteenth birthday.

LIEUTENANT RAYMOND A. MITCHELL

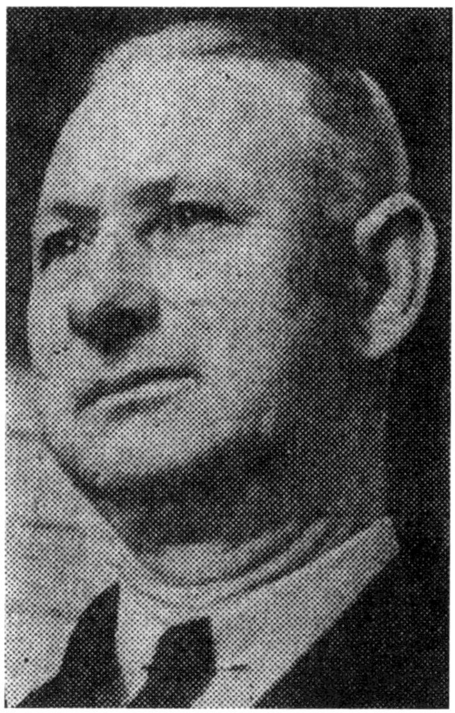

Lieutenant Raymond A. Mitchell, forty-eight, Engine Company 4. *Brockton Fire Museum.*

Raymond A. Mitchell was born on March 6, 1893, in Bath, Maine. By 1900, he was living in Brockton, Massachusetts, with his grandparents Willet and Margaret Agers. In 1914, he married Junie Packer. The couple lived at 7 Martin Street and had two sons: Raymond Allen (born June 14, 1926) and Clayton Stanley (born October 4, 1927). The *Brockton Enterprise* reported that June and Raymond were a happy couple who spent every moment together when Raymond was not at work. They liked to entertain and loved to attend old-fashioned dances.

Appointed to the Brockton Fire Department on August 12, 1918, Mitchell was assigned to Engine 1 on August 12, 1918, and transferred to Engine 4 on March 19, 1919.

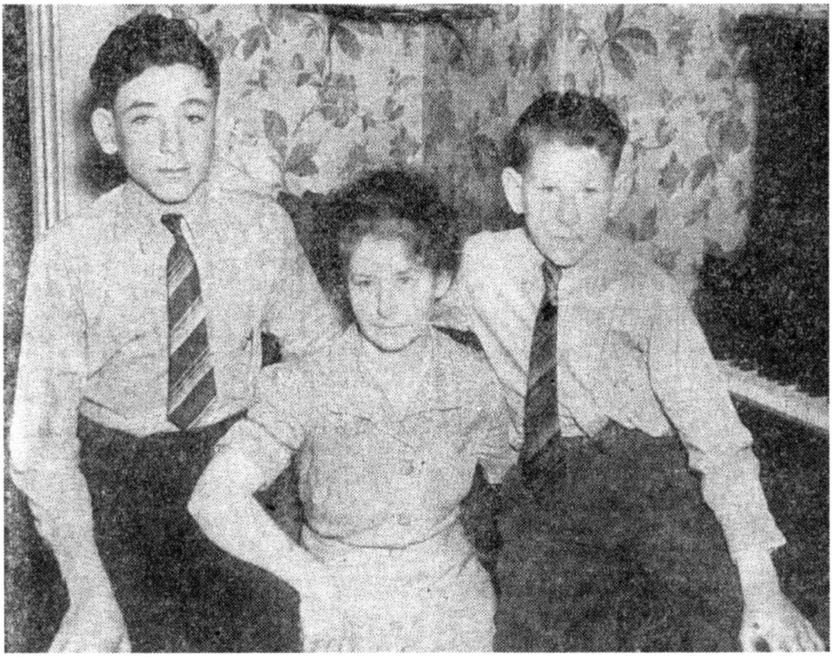

Junie Mitchell learned of her husband's death when a reporter visited her home. She is pictured with her sons, Raymond A. (*left*) and Clayton S. (*right*), at their home. *Brockton Fire Museum.*

He was promoted to lieutenant on November 18, 1939, and assigned to Engine 4. Mitchell kept fit by attending noon classes at the YMCA.

Mitchell was killed during the second collapse. After the first collapse, the *Enterprise* reported Lieutenant Mitchell had been speaking to police Sergeant Timothy O'Brien, whose brother Daniel was also fighting the fire. Sergeant O'Brien asked if Lieutenant Mitchell had seen his brother. Mitchell replied, "No, I haven't" and turned and walked back into the balcony. A minute later, the second collapse occurred, and Lieutenant Mitchell was crushed to death. Sadly, Junie Mitchell had not heard of her husband's death until visited by an *Enterprise* reporter that morning. Her sons had already left for their day at the Paine School and were summoned home only an hour into their day.

Lieutenant Mitchell's funeral was held the Wednesday after the fire at the Hickey Funeral Home and conducted by Reverend Edwin H. Gibson of the First Parish Congregational Church. Burial was at Union Cemetery. Bearers from the fire department included Captain Totman, R.J. Barry, R. Hurd, Lieutenant Papineau, Captain D. Lone and Lieutenant Seavy. Junie Mitchell received a $1,000 annuity until her death in 1944. The boys received a $200 annuity until their eighteenth birthdays. Both boys would follow in their father's footsteps and become Brockton firefighters. Raymond would rise through the ranks and retire as a captain.

MATTHEW MCGEARY

Firefighter Matthew McGeary was born in Brockton on July 5, 1891. On January 20, 1920, he was appointed to the Brockton Fire Department at the age of twenty-eight and later detailed to Engine 3 on February 2, 1920. On April 11, 1927, he was shifted to Ladder 3, where he served for the remainder of his career. Prior to his appointment to the fire department, McGeary worked in the shoe industry. The 1910 federal census lists him as a shoe finisher at the age of nineteen. His draft registration card completed on June 5, 1917, states that he served three years in the National Guard. He did not serve in World War I, and the 1920 federal census indicates that he changed jobs sometime between 1917 and his appointment to the fire department, during which time he worked as a sexton for a Catholic church in Bridgewater.

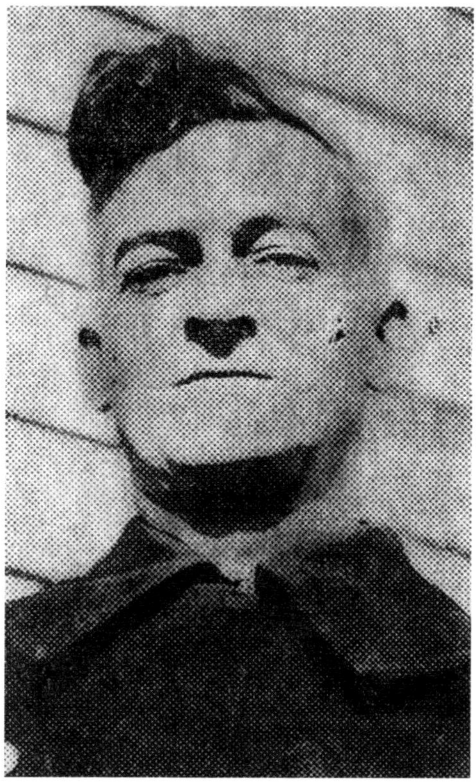

Firefighter Matthew E. McGeary, forty-nine, Ladder Company 3. *Brockton Fire Museum.*

McGeary married Nora C. Clifford on August 31, 1911, at the age of twenty. The couple lived at 83 Ford Street and had three children. Their eldest child, Mary Alice, was born on August 19, 1914. The second child, Matthew E. McGeary Jr., was born in 1917 but died in 1922. Their third child, Irving A. McGeary, was born on January

24, 1922. McGeary was a popular man in the department. The *Enterprise* reported after his death that he was known as one of those always ready to take a dangerous task in firefighting. The paper also reported that he was a religious man who went to church every morning. In addition to being a member of St. Edward's Church in Brockton, he was a member of the Third Order of St. Francis and a member of the Legion of Mary. He also made numerous retreats at St. Francis Friary in Brookline, Massachusetts.

It was this strong sense of faith that helped his widow cope. Visited by the *Enterprise* the day of the fire, she recalled they had spoken the night of the fire. When she said goodbye, he told her, "Never say goodbye, Nora, Good-Night." In addition to his wife and children, McGeary left three brothers, including his brother James, who was a firefighter at Station 3 and also worked the Strand Theatre fire.

McGeary's funeral was held on Wednesday, March 12, 1941, at St. Edward's Church. A High Mass of Requiem was sung by the Reverend Joseph D. Meredith with burial following at Calvary Cemetery. Firemen Harry J. Belmore, Albert E. Grady, Lieutenant James F. Toomey, James McAuliffe, Chester W. Bell, Walter S. Rozum and Charles W. J. Carter served as bearers.

Nora McGeary lived until 1974, receiving an annuity of $1,000. Irving received an annuity of $200 until his eighteenth birthday.

WILLIAM J. MURPHY

William J. Murphy dreamed of becoming a firefighter from the time he was a boy. Born in 1911, he was appointed to the fire department on May 24, 1937, and detailed to Ladder 2 at that time. He was later transferred to Squad A, where he was serving the day of the Strand fire. The youngest of the thirteen firefighters to lose their lives, Murphy was born and raised in Brockton, growing up only a half a mile from Station 4, located on the East Side of the city at the corner of Crescent and Lyman Streets. His father, John Murphy, was a former welfare officer in the city. The eldest of seven children, Murphy was a devout Catholic and member of St. Coleman's Church, where he served as an altar boy.

Murphy married Grace O'Neil of neighboring Easton in 1939, and the couple resided at 5 Kingman Avenue. On Sunday, March 9, 1941, before William left for his long and ultimately last shift at Squad A, the couple attended the 7:00 a.m. Mass at St. Coleman's. His rosary beads were found on his bed in the fire station when relatives went to retrieve his belongings, possibly being used when the first alarm rang.

Murphy was found near Captain Carroll in the wreckage on the main floor and was the second body to be recovered. An excellent hoseman, he was remembered by friends and family as having a funny and fun-loving disposition and as being devoted to firefighting, his only hobby being the study of firefighting methods and collecting fire scene photos. He and his wife had no children.

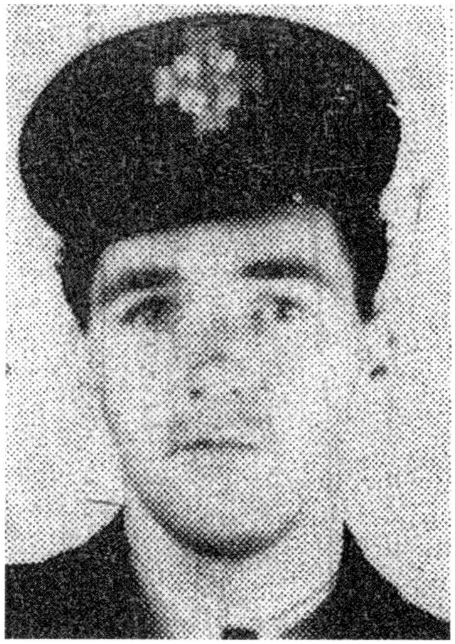

Firefighter William J. Murphy, twenty-nine, Squad A. *Brockton Fire Museum.*

Murphy was waked from his parents' home at 94 Kingman Street. Mass was celebrated by Reverend Edward J. McKenna, assistant pastor at St. Coleman's Church. Bearers included firemen William J. Murphy, John F. Kelley, Fred M. Grady, Allan A. Minnehan, Harold L. Weeks, Lawrence Johnson and Edward L. Burrell. He is buried at Calvary Cemetery in Brockton.

DANIEL C. O'BRIEN

Daniel Christopher O'Brien was born in Brockton on December 12, 1894. Before his appointment to the Brockton Fire Department on January 26, 1920, he worked in the shoe industry in the city. During World War I, he served in the U.S. Army. After the war, in 1919, he married Alice Rudden. The couple lived at 35 Division Street and had two children: Margaret (born circa 1921) and Daniel (born circa 1924).

Firefighter O'Brien was known as a "front-line" man among his buddies. After his appointment to the fire department, he was assigned to Engine 4 on February 2, 1920. He shifted to Ladder 1 on March 19, 1924, and then to Squad A on March 26, 1935. He was a regular communicant at St.

Edward's Church and a member of the American Legion and Holy Name Society.

He called home that Sunday night to tell his family, "It has been a quiet day, and I'll see you in the morning." Sadly, he would die when the balcony collapsed and was later found in the back orchestra seats. His brother, Timothy O'Brien, a police sergeant, was also on duty that night and assisted in the rescue efforts. At one point, he was told to leave because it was unclear where his brother was.

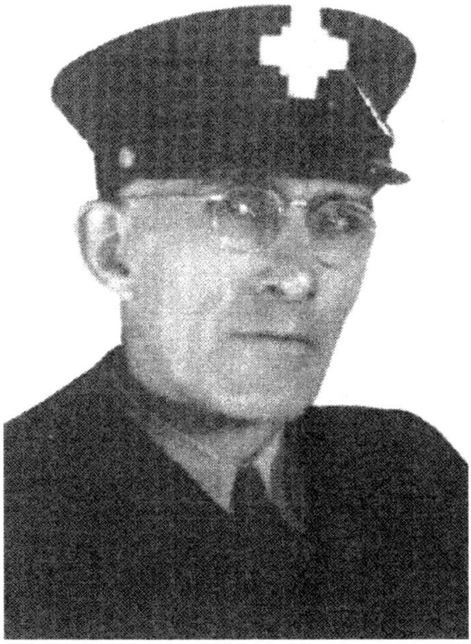

Firefighter Daniel C. O'Brien, forty-five, Squad A. *Brockton Fire Museum.*

In addition to his brother, wife and children, O'Brien left behind his widowed elderly mother, Sabina O'Brien, who was eighty-four. During the wake held at O'Brien's house, Sabina sat at the foot of his casket and kept vigil at his side until his burial. Overcome by grief, O'Brien's mother, daughter and brother were attended to by a physician neighbor and friend of the family, Dr. John E. Cahill. The next day, Thursday, March 13, 1941, a full military funeral took place with a High Mass of Requiem sung at St. Edward's Church with burial at Calvary Cemetery. Bearers from the fire department included Frank M. Kennedy, Lieutenant Papineau, William F. McKenney, John T. Moran, Robert F. Murray and George F. Doherty.

Among his belongings at the fire station, a rosary was discovered on his cot with a Chesterfield wrapper between two beads. When his wife received them, she quipped, "So he couldn't even keep from smoking in his last rosary." Daniel O'Brien had not been well and was considering the need for stomach surgery, the prospect of which had led him to promise his wife he would make an effort to reduce his smokes per day. Alice O'Brien received a $1,000 annuity until her death in 1948. His son, Daniel, received a $200 annuity until his eighteenth birthday.[40]

DENIS P. MURPHY

Born in Killarney, Ireland, in 1892, Denis P. Murphy immigrated to the United States in 1895. On November 18, 1918, Murphy was appointed to the Brockton Fire Department and assigned to Engine 5 on March 19, 1919. He transferred to Engine 1 on February 2, 1920, and was serving with Squad A on the day of the Strand Theatre fire.

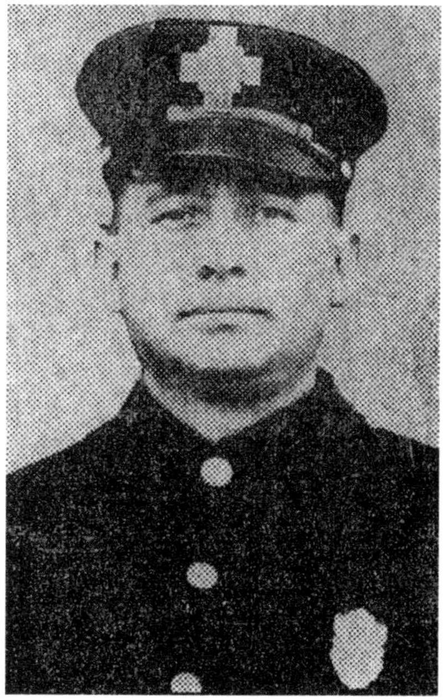

Firefighter Denis P. Murphy, forty-nine, Squad A. *Brockton Fire Museum.*

Married to Mary Sullivan, the couple lived at 551 Warren Avenue and had three sons: Thomas Joseph, nineteen; Robert, eighteen; and Edward, thirteen. Thomas and Robert were students at Tufts College in Boston, Robert having been president and class orator of Brockton High School's class of 1940.

Firefighter Murphy was described in the *Brockton Enterprise* as a quiet man with a happy and cheerful nature beloved by all who knew him. He was a member of St. Patrick's Church and regularly received communion. His wake was held from his home and a solemn High Mass celebrated at St. Patrick's Church before burial at Calvary Cemetery. Mass was celebrated by Reverend Thomas J. Murphy, SJ, a cousin of the deceased, with Reverend Lawrence P. Morrisroe, who gave last rites to Murphy as he lay buried in the debris, serving as deacon. Bearers were friends and included a cousin, Judge Maurice J. Murphy, as well as John Ennis, Joseph Courtney, Daniel Sullivan, Michael Sullivan and Maurice B. Murphy.

During the wake, firemen from Brockton's Station 2 answered a call for a garage fire almost directly across the street from the Murphy home. Murphy's wife and sons were in the front hallway of their home receiving condolences from friends and relatives when fire apparatus arrived on scene. Nerves frayed, the family was taken to other parts of the home to regain their composure until the situation was cleared and the fire and police personnel had departed.

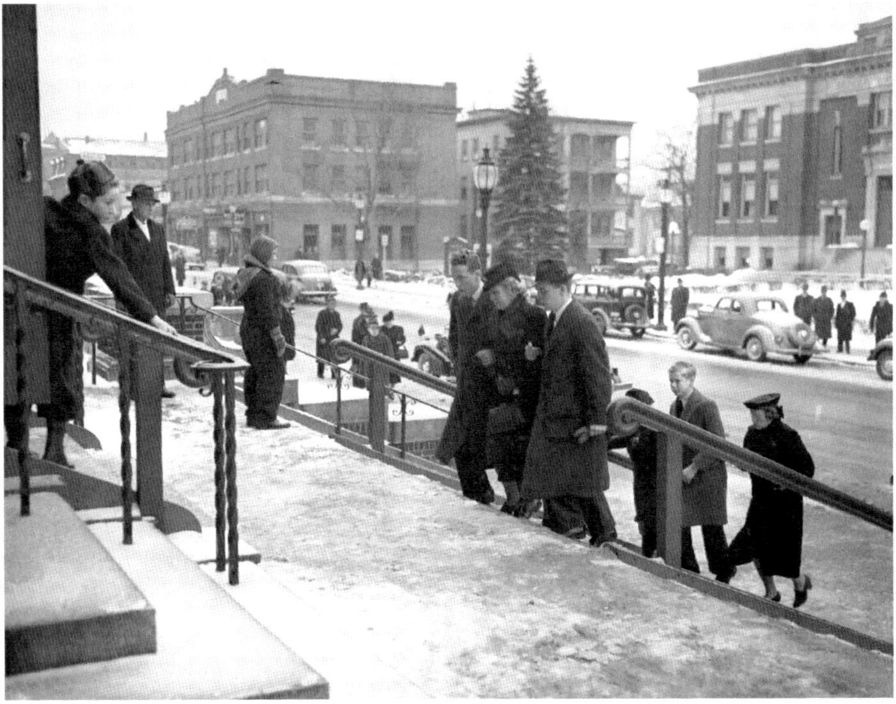

Mary Murphy, widow of firefighter Denis Murphy, was escorted into her husband's funeral Mass at St. Patrick's Church by her sons, Robert and Joseph, March 12, 1941. *Bauman Collection, Stonehill College.*

His widow received a $1,000 annuity and youngest son, Edward, a $200 annuity until his eighteenth birthday.

Roy A. McKeraghan

Roy McKeraghan was born in Brockton on October 6, 1898. Before his appointment to the Brockton Fire Department on June 18, 1934, he worked as a chauffeur at E.C. Hall Company. He and his wife, Mabel, were married around 1918 and lived at 76 Green Place with their two children. Their eldest son, Roy Andrew Jr., was born on November 2, 1919. Their youngest son, Richard, was born on June 10, 1932. Only eight when his father died, Richard would eventually follow in his father's footsteps and join the Brockton Fire Department in the 1950s.

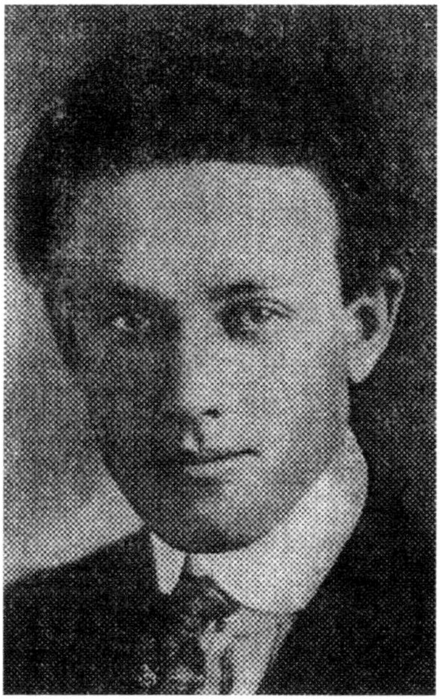

Firefighter Roy A. McKeraghan, forty-two, Squad A. *Brockton Fire Museum.*

McKeraghan was a member of Squad A. Upon hearing the news of his death, McKeraghan's wife became hysterical, and the police and a physician were summoned. She was strapped down and received injections to make her sleep. Her son, Roy, a private first class in the U.S. Army, stationed at Camp Edwards, stayed at her side. He was scheduled to be married that Friday, March 15, 1941, to Avis Olson of Brockton. The wedding would be postponed to March 22, 1941.

McKeraghan's funeral took place the Thursday after the fire. Services were held in the Sampson Funeral Home by Reverend L.W. Kellie, pastor of the Warren Avenue Baptist Church. Bells rang as his funeral procession passed the Campello Station on its way to Pine Hill Cemetery in West Bridgewater. Engine 2, Ladder 2 and Combination 2 were pulled out of the station, and the officers in the front stood at attention, eyes front and heads up even though their tears ran. The hearse passed by with three firefighters on each side. As the bells faded, the men said their final goodbyes, and apparatus were backed slowly into the station and the doors shut. Bearers from the fire department included Captain J.D. McCarthy, Captain Arthur M. Which, A.C. Larson, Jesse R. Cole, William J. Yancy and T.F. Jones.

McKeraghan's widow was still under the care of a physician and did not attend her husband's funeral. Mabel McKeraghan received a $1,000 annuity and his son Richard a $200 annuity until his eighteenth birthday.

FREDERICK F. KELLEY

Born in Haverhill, Massachusetts, on April 5, 1892, Frederick F. Kelley worked as a shoe cutter before and after World War I. During the war, he served eighteen months overseas as an army combat engineer assigned to Company A, Second Division, in France. He was also a semiprofessional catcher who played for the Haverhill Shamrocks of the city of Haverhill team and the Winchell Company team of the Haverhill Shoe Shop League.

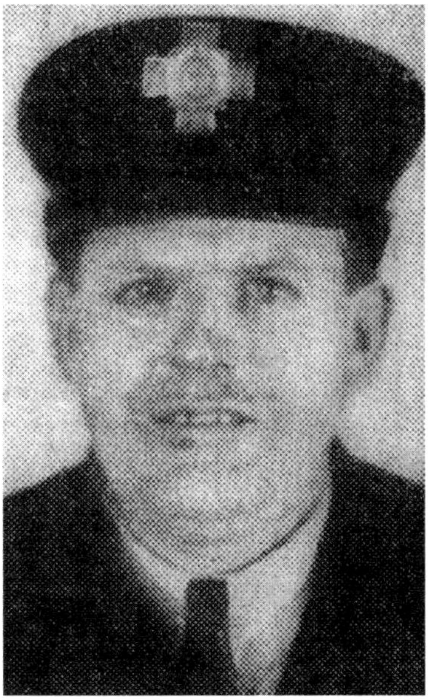

Firefighter Frederick F. Kelley, forty-eight, Engine Company 1. *Brockton Fire Museum.*

Appointed to the Brockton Fire Department on November 8, 1926, Kelley was assigned to Engine Company 1. On March 10, 1941, he was off duty but called to respond to the second alarm at the Strand Theatre fire. Kelley was hurt in several fires during his career but never seriously. He was killed on the balcony when the roof of the theater collapsed, and his body was the last to be recovered from the wreckage.

Kelley married Margaret Calnan in 1923. The couple lived at 37 Exchange Street and had two children: Robert, born on February 26, 1924, and

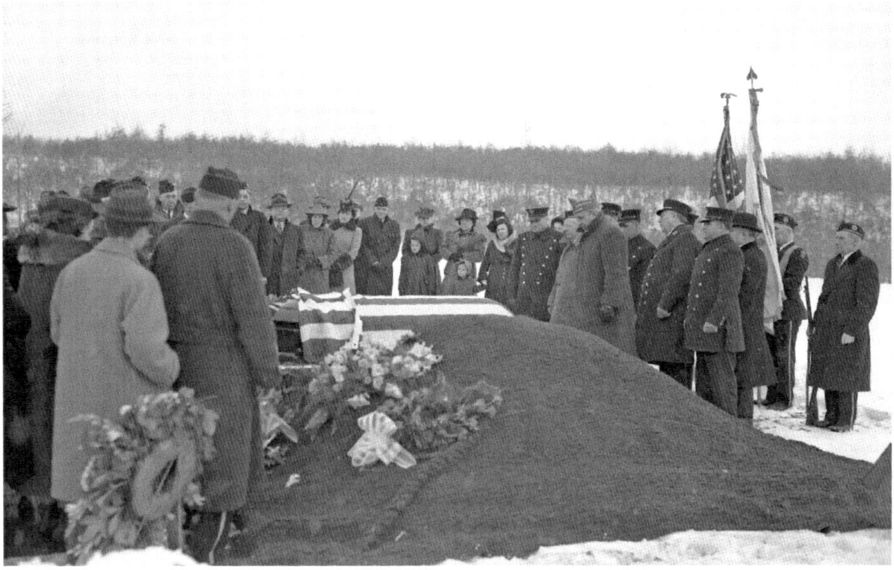

Reverend Joseph Kennedy of St. Patrick's Parish is shown reading the committal service at the Calvary Cemetery grave of war veteran and fallen firefighter Frederick F. Kelley, March 13, 1941. *Bauman Collection, Stonehill College.*

Frederick, born on September 25, 1925. Both boys had gone to school the day of the fire. Frederick, a student at St. Patrick's School, was told by a nun to go home. His brother, Robert, a junior at Brockton High School, was also sent home. Upon arrival, they were told by their mother their father had been killed.

Buried with full military honors, Kelley was remembered as a prominent athlete, active in baseball, bicycle racing and bowling circles. His funeral was held at St. Patrick's Church with Mass sung by Reverend Lawrence P. Morrisroe, assisted by Reverend Joseph Kenney as deacon and Reverend Jeremiah Minihan as subdeacon. Burial was at Calvary Cemetery. Serving as bearers from the fire department were Captain Daniel Long, Henry Minnehan, Timothy Quill, Frank Kennedy, William Kuplast and George Robillard. His widow, Margaret, received a $1,000 annuity and died in 1979. Their sons each received a $200 annuity. Robert, who died in 2013, told his daughter that his saddest memory was retrieving his father's belongings. He went by himself to the fire station to clean out his father's locker and brought home his father's personal belongings. He was unable to get his father's badge, which always bothered him.[41]

GEORGE A. COLLINS

George A. Collins was the eldest of the firefighters killed in the Strand Theatre fire. Born in Wardsboro, Vermont, on January 29, 1879, he was sixty-two when he died. It is unknown when and why he first came to Brockton, but he is listed as a painter in the 1900 census. In 1903, he and his first wife, Ella Oldham Howard, had a son, Howard L. Collins. The couple divorced, and Collins married Elva Woodcock on September 11, 1909. It is unknown if his second wife died or if they divorced, but Collins married his third wife, Bess Williams, around 1922. The couple lived at 19 Wilmington Street.

Appointed to the fire department on December 12, 1917, he was a member of Engine Company 1. Buried in the collapse of the Strand balcony, he was identified by a Hamler pocket watch, a wristwatch, auto keys and glasses. He was also wearing a truss for a rupture. He was survived by his wife, Bess, and son, Howard, a lieutenant commander aboard the USS *Dorsey*, who was stationed in Honolulu, Hawaii, at the time of his father's death. The *Dorsey* was out at sea on December 7, 1941, escaping the attack on Pearl Harbor. Lieutenant Commander Collins died in 1984.

George Collins's funeral service was held at the Sampson Funeral Home, with Reverend Edwin H. Gibson, pastor of the First Parish Congregational Church officiating. No formal bearers were present, although many of his fellow firefighters attended the service. His body was cremated at Forest Hills, and a gravestone bears his and his widow's names in Island Pond Cemetery, Ludlow, Massachusetts. Bess Collins received a $1,000 annuity until her death on December 10, 1977.

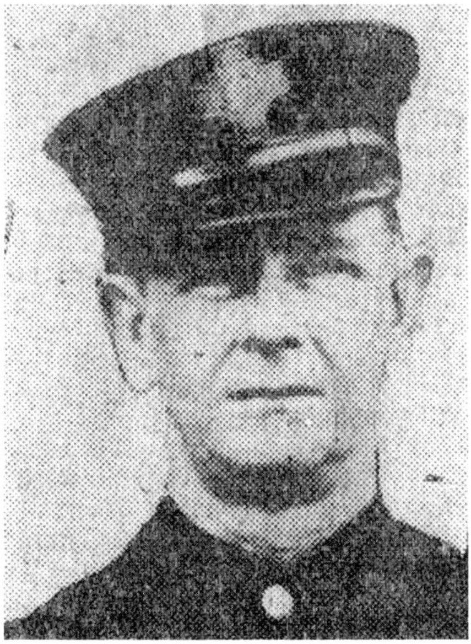

Firefighter George A. Collins, sixty-two, Engine Company 1. *Brockton Fire Museum.*

HENRY E. SULLIVAN

Henry Sullivan and John Malcolm McNeill were best friends who lived next door to each other and worked the same shift. They walked to work together and were found less than two feet apart in the wreckage of the Strand Theatre. Born in Holbrook on May 23, 1895, Sullivan served with the U.S. Army on battlefields in France during World War I. After the war, he settled in Brockton, working in the shoe industry and marrying Mary Murphy around 1922. Sullivan was appointed to the Brockton fire department on May 3, 1930, and assigned to Squad A. On April 16, 1932, he was transferred from Squad A to Engine 1. Before leaving for work on that fateful day, Sullivan went to Mass at 6:30 a.m. He returned home and drove his wife to Mass because the weather was bad. That was the last time she saw her husband alive. Mary Sullivan was holding her crystal rosaries her husband had given her for Christmas saying "her beads" when she received the news that her husband was one of the men trapped and killed when the Strand Theatre roof collapsed.

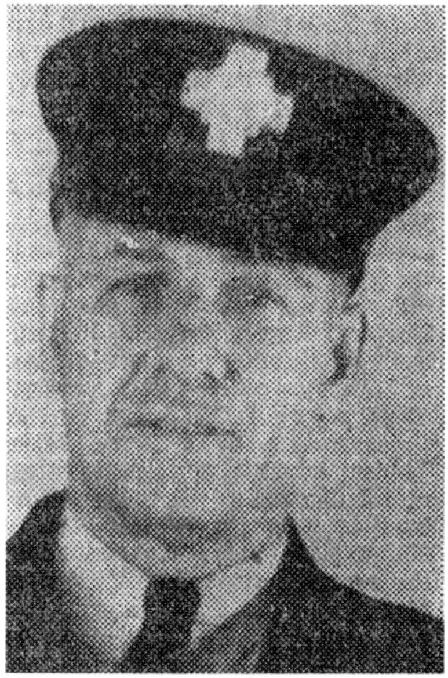

Firefighter Henry E. Sullivan, forty-five, Engine Company 1. *Brockton Fire Museum.*

The couple had been planning a trip to Washington with their two girls during Sullivan's summer vacation, which was to be a graduation present to their eldest daughter, Madelyn, who would graduate from Brockton High School in June 1941. Each year, they would make a trip to Benson's Wild Animal Farm in Hudson, New Hampshire, and were often seen packing for a day trip to the beach during Sullivan's days off in the summer.

Henry Sullivan loved his home and family. He loved to work around the house, fixing things and planting trees for shade. He was also fond of sitting in the living room or outside on the glider smoking his pipe. His greatest pride was polishing his car, and one of the most familiar sights on Mulberry Street was Henry with a grease gun under his car. According to his grandson Michael Sites, that night was to be Sullivan's last tour of duty before transferring to the Fire Alarm Division.

Rites for Sullivan were held at St. Edward's Church, with John J. Flynn singing the Mass and the burial following at St. Patrick's Cemetery in Brockton. Bearers included William H. Sweeney, Axel C. Larson, Arthur T. Williams, Andrew Johnson, Lieutenant James M. Ryan and Byron F. Vinton.

Sullivan's widow, Mary, received a $1,000 annuity, which helped her pay off her home. The couple's youngest daughter, Rose Marie, fourteen, received a $200 annuity. The eldest daughter, Madelyn, eighteen, did not receive an annuity. Mary Sullivan died in Brockton on November 15, 1970.

MARTIN E. LIPPER

Martin E. Lipper was born on November 9, 1894, in Brockton. He served in the U.S. Navy from 1917 until 1921. Before entering the service, he worked as a conductor for the Bay State Street Railroad Company in Brockton. He

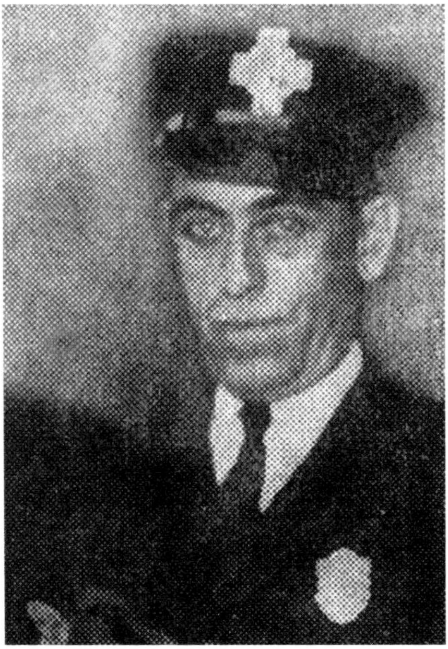

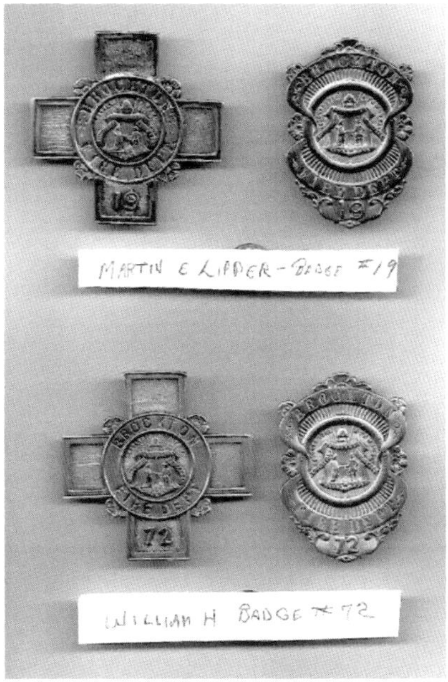

Left: Firefighter Martin E. Lipper, forty-six, Engine Company 1. *Brockton Fire Museum.*

Right: The badges of Martin L. Lipper, killed in the Strand fire, and his brother William H. Lipper, injured in the fire, have been kept by the family. Not all families were given the badges of their fallen loved ones. In fact, some badge numbers are still being used today. *Courtesy of William Lipper, son of William H. Lipper.*

served in the navy during World War I and was appointed to the Brockton Fire Department on July 19, 1926. On July 24, 1927, he was assigned to Engine 1. He shifted to Squad A on April 11, 1927, but rejoined Engine 1 on March 19, 1929, where he served until his death.

Described as being quiet and a homebody, his friendly nature made him a favorite with those who knew him. He married Emily Martin in 1932. Emily worked as a skiver in the shoe industry. The *Brockton Enterprise* reported that he said a cheerful "See you in the morning" to his wife as she left him at the Pleasant Street Station on Sunday at noon, after bringing him his lunch and stopping for a visit as she customarily did on his long day of duty.

The couple lived at 21 Forest Avenue and had no children, but Martin left behind two brothers and two sisters. One of his brothers, William, was also a firefighter and on duty at the Strand. William was injured when the roof caved in and his safety belt got caught while he tried to slip through a hole to the floor below. After wiggling free, he returned to search for his brother. He was treated for injuries at the scene of the fire. Reflecting on the aftermath of the fire, Lipper's nephew remembers coming down the stairs the morning of the fire and seeing his mother sitting crying at the telephone holding his brother Paul. The call had been from someone telling his mother that her husband had died at the scene and Martin Lipper was injured. The reverse was true, but his mother did not receive this news until later that day.

Martin Lipper was identified by his boot, which included his initials, M.E.L., and his stature. In addition to his duties as a fireman, he also served as a director and member of the auditing committee of the Brockton Fireman's Credit Union. He received a military funeral with a Mass at St. Patrick's Church celebrated by Reverend Jeremiah Minihan with Reverend Lawrence Morrisroe as deacon and Reverend Joseph W. Kenney as subdeacon. Bearers included firemen Harry J. Belmore, Albert E. Grady, Charles W. Williams, Carl E. Johnson, Stanley Krance and Jessie R. Cole.

His widow would receive an annuity payment of $1,000, continue her work in the shoe industry and later move to and buy a house in Avon, Massachusetts, where she died on July 23, 1977.

JOHN M. MCNEILL

John Malcom McNeill was born in Randolph, Massachusetts, on December 9, 1896, to John B. and Mary E. McNeill. His father was a blacksmith with his own shop and later served as town treasurer. After serving in the navy's transport service during World War I, McNeill went to work as a shoe cutter until his appointment to the Brockton Fire Department and detail to Squad A on October 31, 1927. He transferred to Ladder 1 on March 26, 1935, and Ladder 2 on November 1, 1937, before returning to Ladder 1. Alice LaLiberte Bruce remembers that, as children, she and the other neighborhood kids would go and watch the firemen answer a call, and McNeill would wave as he passed driving the back of the ladder truck in the tiller seat.

Known as Malcolm, nickname "Mal," firefighter McNeill and his wife, Anna Louise Riley, lived at 35 Mulberry Street in the Irish section of Brockton, known as the "Tip." The couple married on October 23, 1919, and had five children. A deeply religious man, McNeill attended St. Edward's Church but often would call his wife to say he would be late because he was going to stop for a few moments of prayer at St. Theresa's, the Syrian church near the station, on his way home from work.

Father Joseph Meredith of St. Edward's Church brought the news of McNeill's death to his wife, Anna. When he arrived, Meredith asked the

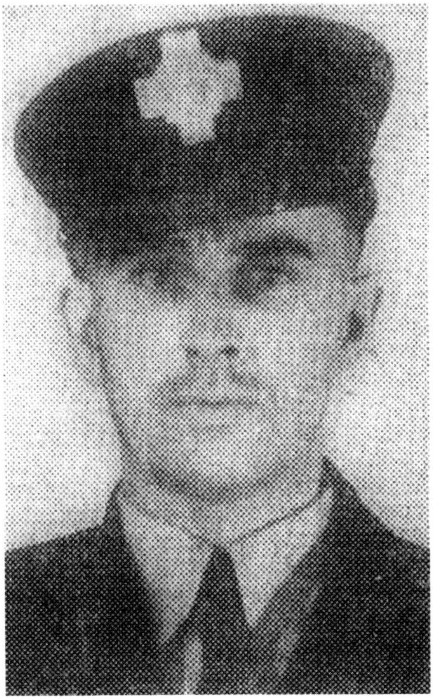

Firefighter John M. McNeill, forty-three, Ladder Company 1. *Brockton Fire Museum.*

McNeills' youngest daughter, Muriel, if she "had been a good girl, just as her daddy had been a good man." When she looked at him in bewilderment, and before she could answer, he said, "Soon you will be old enough to make your first communion, offer it for your father." Anna McNeill, sitting near her daughter, knew even before he could give her the news. It was not the first time she had received bad news about her husband. In 1935, he was badly injured at a two-alarm fire on Ash Street. Suffering from a punctured lung and overexertion, he was out of service for five months. That time, he would return. This time, McNeill left a grief-stricken widow, who remembered sitting in the yard on summer evenings and sending her eldest daughter to the station with his dinner. The car McNeill had just bought sat in the yard waiting for him to get his license that week.

Firefighter McNeill's military funeral was held from J. Frank Conley Funeral Home with a High Mass of Requiem sung at St. Edward's Church by Reverend Lawrence F. Naves of West Newbury. Bearers included firemen Cornelius J. Burke, Roger F. Varnum, Harold D. Shurtleff, Sewell L. Pattangall, Daniel F. Reardon and Walter F. Langley. He is buried in Saint Mary's Cemetery in Randolph. His widow, Anna, received a $1,000 annuity until her death on January 12, 1978. McNeill's children Barbara, seventeen; Robert, fifteen; and Muriel, six, received $200 annuities until their eighteenth birthdays. His other two children—Mary Louis, twenty-one, and John Joseph, nineteen—were too old for the annuity.

BARTHOLOMEW HERLIHY

Firefighter Bartholomew Herlihy was born in Brockton on May 13, 1895. He was appointed to the Brockton Fire Department on January 26, 1920. On February 1, 1920, he was assigned to Ladder 1 at Central Fire Station in Brockton. He remained with that company throughout his twenty-one-year term of service with the department. Prior to his appointment with the fire department, Herlihy served in the army, first in 1916 for four months during the border war with Mexico and then during World War I with D Company, 101st Infantry, AEF. Before World War I, he worked in the shoe industry. After the war and before his appointment to the fire department, Herlihy worked as a steamfitter.

The same year he joined the fire department, Herlihy married Ethel Lillian McGowan. The couple had two children: Ralph L. (born 1921) and Marie H. (born 1925). He was known as a crack ladderman and had escaped serious injuries in 1939 in the opera house fire when he was pulled to safety by a fellow firefighter just as a section of the flooring gave way. Two years later, however, he did not escape danger, being one of the firefighters on the balcony of the Strand Theatre when the roof collapsed. Herlihy was found alive in the rubble and brought to the Brockton Hospital. One of the first rescued, he was also the most seriously injured, with both a crushed chest and spine injuries. Newspapers reported his condition as "not expected to live." The *Brockton Enterprise* reported receiving over one hundred calls about "Private Bart's," condition. He died two days after the fire on March 12, 1941, never regaining consciousness, with his wife and two children at his side.

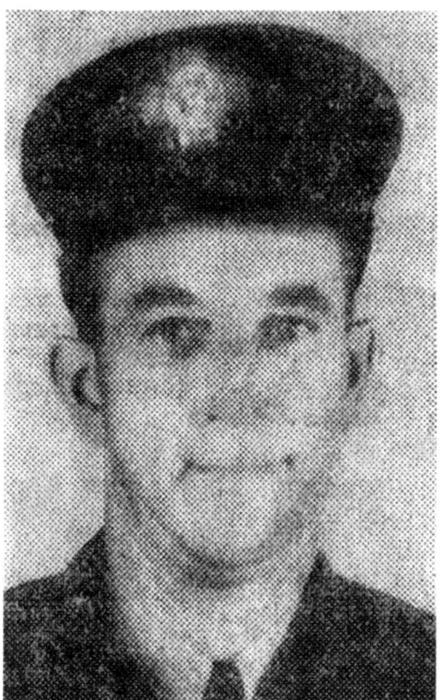

Firefighter Bartholomew Herlihy, forty-five, Ladder Company 1. *Brockton Fire Museum.*

As was custom, his belongings were gathered together from his locker on Thursday. That was when his comrades, Roger Varnum and Fred Grady made a sad discovery. On a shelf in the locker, they found an old program with names written on the back. The names were of firemen he would call to substitute for him. The program was from "The Strand Theatre."[42]

Firefighter Herlihy's funeral was held from his residence at 22 West Park Street on Saturday, March 15, 1941. A solemn High Mass of Requiem was celebrated at St. Patrick's Church by Reverend Joseph W. Kenney, with Lawrence P. Morrisroe, deacon, and Reverend Jeremiah Minihan, subdeacon. Active bearers from the fire department included Captain Daniel Long, Lieutenant James F. Toomey (a close friend who had donated blood to Herlihy when he was first admitted to the hospital, even though he himself was also injured), Lieutenant Frederick M. Papineau, Cornelius Burke, Roger L. Varnum and Walter F. McLaren. Captain Charles G. McCarthy led a detail of uniformed firemen marching as escort. The group included Captain Joseph D. McCarthy, Chester Carlson, Walter Braley, Elton Hoxie, Frank Kennedy, Ralph Williams, Frank Currier, William Haverty, Leonard Newton, Harry Belmore, William Stack, George Doherty, John Coughlin, Daniel Reardon, George Brady, Leo O'Brien, Fred Peck, John Dineen, John Hamilton, Albert Grady, Eric Nordeen, Fred Grady, Carl Johnson, Edward Burrell, Walter Langley, Harold Weeks, Robert Campbell and Richard Barry.

Herlihy's widow Ethel received a $1,000 annuity until her death in 1952. His daughter, Mary, received a $200 annuity until her eighteenth birthday in 1943. His son, Ralph, was nineteen at the time of his father's death and therefore did not receive any payments.

THE STRAND THEATRE FIRE reduced the Brockton fire force by over 30 percent, and even as the city mourned, it needed a full roster of men to continue to protect the city. Things began to return to normal—or as normal as things can be following such a tragedy—and in the process, the vacant positions were filled by volunteers from other towns, as well as retired Brockton firefighters returning to duty to make certain the city was protected. On Monday, March 17, 1941, at its meeting, the city council confirmed without a dissenting vote to appoint twelve men as replacements for the thirteen who died. The names were submitted by Chief Dickinson to Mayor Rowe. So that the men could begin as soon as possible, appointment rules were suspended, and the men became firemen immediately. No new men were instantly appointed to replace those injured and unable to work. It was assumed that those shifts were filled by those able to work. New appointments included John Kelley, who would replace Captain John Carroll; Anthony Yushkaitis, who would replace Lieutenant Raymond A. Mitchell; and Michael Principe, who would stand in the stead of George Collins. Arthur Perry would fill the boots of Frederick Kelley. Edwin Donahue would replace Martin Lipper, Wallace Campbell would replace Roy McKeraghan, Edward Martin would replace Matthew McGeary and Peter Yuskevicz would replace Malcolm McNeill. Kenneth White replaced young William Murphy, Daniel Buckley replaced Denis Murphy, John Costigan replaced Daniel O'Brien and Lawrence Marston replaced Henry Sullivan. The only position not filled immediately was Bartholomew Herlihy's. John F. Grigas was appointed later to that vacancy. In addition, because two officers were killed, two men would receive promotions. Lieutenant James F. Toomey was promoted to captain, and Joseph P. Murphy was promoted to lieutenant.

5
Honor and Remembrance

Firemen's Disaster Relief Committee Fund

Even before the last of the fallen were removed from the wreckage of the Strand Theatre, the call came to set up a fund for the widows and children of the firemen killed. Throughout the day on Monday, March 10, 1941, the *Enterprise* fielded calls from citizens wanting to know where they could send "money to aid the widows and children of the dead firemen." At noon the day after the fire, the mayor organized a group to be known as the "Mayor's fireman's disaster relief committee" to accept and control contributions. Edward A. Dinneen, manager at the Metropolitan Life Insurance Company in the city, was named as chairman. Other members included Mayor Fred D. Rowe, chairman ex officio; Harold W. Austin, president of the city council; Fred Gurney, president of the Rotary Club; Americus Giannini, president of the Kiwanis Club; Dr. John W. Corbett, president of the Lions Club; Alphonse Samson, president of the Brotherhood of Shoe and Allied Craftsmen; Ethel B. Atwood, president of the Woman's Club of Brockton; John S. Mara, commander of Brockton Post, American Legion; Philomena DiPasqua, president of the Twentieth Century Catholic Club; Charles E. Corcoran, president of the chamber of commerce; Louis Rautenberg, president of the YMHA (Young Men's Hebrew Association); Thomas Wilkinson, president of the Central Labor

Union; Joseph Messier, news editor of the *Brockton Enterprise*; and Joseph Noone, publisher of the *Brockton Union*.[43]

Before the committee could take its first action, three Brockton citizens visited Chief Dickinson and gave $10 bills, and several pledges had been received, including $1,000 from Howard Johnson stores. The committee's first action was the designation of four key reception areas for funds and offers of aid to be collected. These included the Mayor's Office, Brockton National Bank, Home National Bank and the *Brockton Enterprise* offices. On Wednesday, March 12, 1941, the *Brockton Enterprise* reported the fund had already raised $5,000, and additional contribution areas had been added, including Brockton and People's Savings Banks, Federal Savings and Loan Association, Campello Cooperative Bank and Montello Federal Loan Association. Wednesday was also designated as an official day of mourning for the city, with all school, city offices and businesses closed until 6:00 p.m. Ten of the twelve funerals were held Wednesday, with the remaining two slated for Thursday. Bartholomew Herlihy, who died from his injuries on Wednesday evening, was buried on Saturday.

Calls, telegrams and letters of sympathy were received from across the nation, along with offers to help. By Thursday, another $10,000.00 had been received. A tag day was planned for Saturday in the city. To assist with the avalanche of donations, Chairman Dinneen appointed ten volunteer secretaries to "sort, count and tabulate the endless stream of contributions" being received. On March 14, 1941, Stanley Bauman photographed some of these volunteers sorting and tabulating contributions, who included Mary Shepardson, Pearl Stone, Mary Booth, Germaine Dupre, Doris Dahlborg, Margaret Burke and Mary Mitenis. No donation was too small, as shown by that of twelve-year-old Frederick Terry, the youngest of seven children, who contributed his entire life savings of $0.25, which was collected by Chairman Dinneen when Frederick dropped it off at the fund office in city hall. Larger donations included $10.00 from First Lady Eleanor Roosevelt; $10.00 from Brockton's George's Café; $50.00 from Massachusetts governor Leverett Saltonstall; $50.00 from Reno, Nevada firemen; $200.00 from the Needham (Massachusetts) Fire Association; $500.00 from New England Telephone and Telegraph Company; and $1,300.00 from the New England Fire Chiefs Association.

As its contribution to the Fireman's Disaster Relief Committee, the Atherton Furniture Company of Brockton canceled $375 in bills of deceased firemen. Receipted bills for "payment in full" were mailed to the widows on Friday, March 14, 1941. Brockton Hospital officials voted

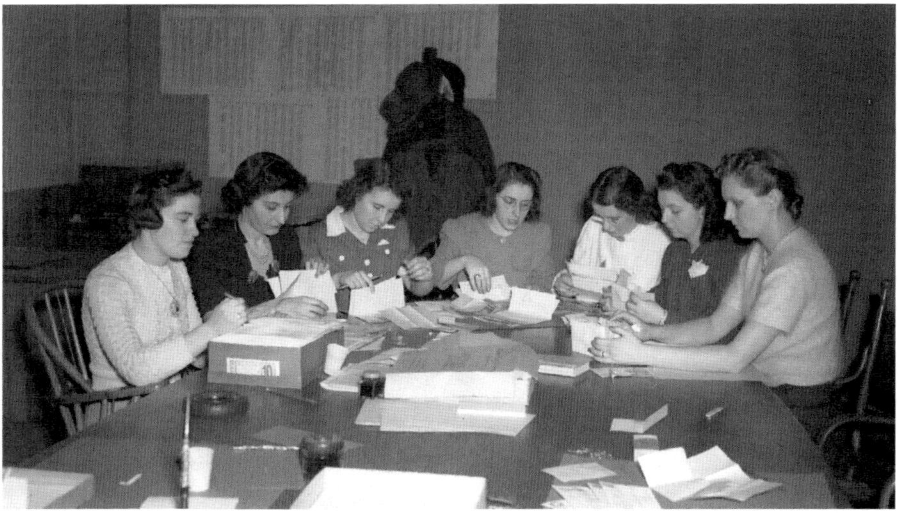

Volunteers sorting and tabulating contributions in the offices of the Firemen's Disaster Fund in Brockton City Hall included *(from left to right)* Mary Shepardson, Pearl Stone, Mary Booth, Germaine Dupre, Doris Dahlborg, Margaret Burke and Mary Mitenis, March 13, 1941. *Bauman Collection, Stonehill College.*

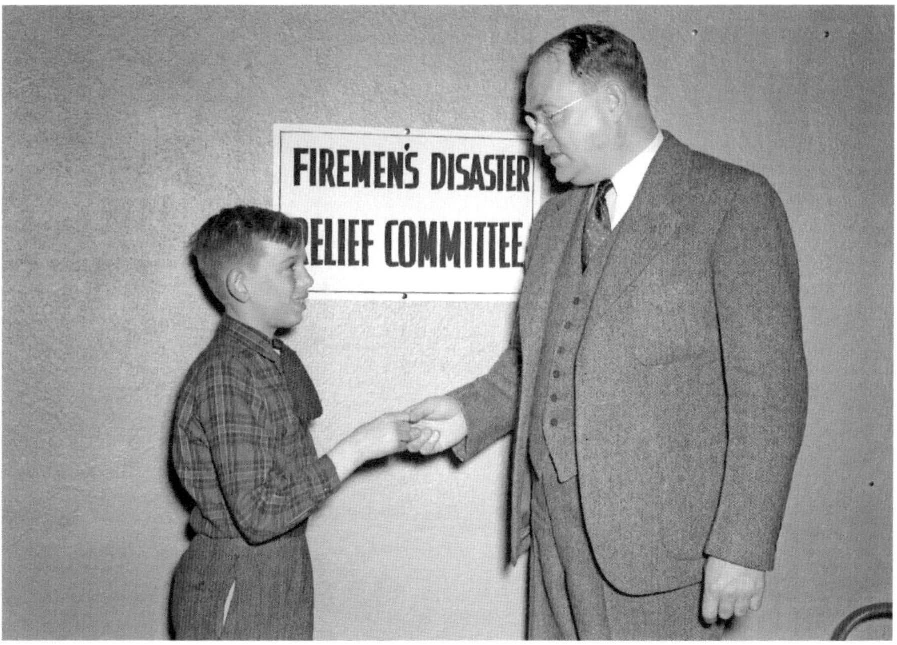

"No Donation Too Small." Twelve-year-old Frederick Terry, the youngest of seven children, contributed his entire life savings of twenty-five cents, which was collected by Chairman Dinneen when Frederick dropped it off at the fund office in Brockton City Hall on March 13, 1941. *Bauman Collection, Stonehill College.*

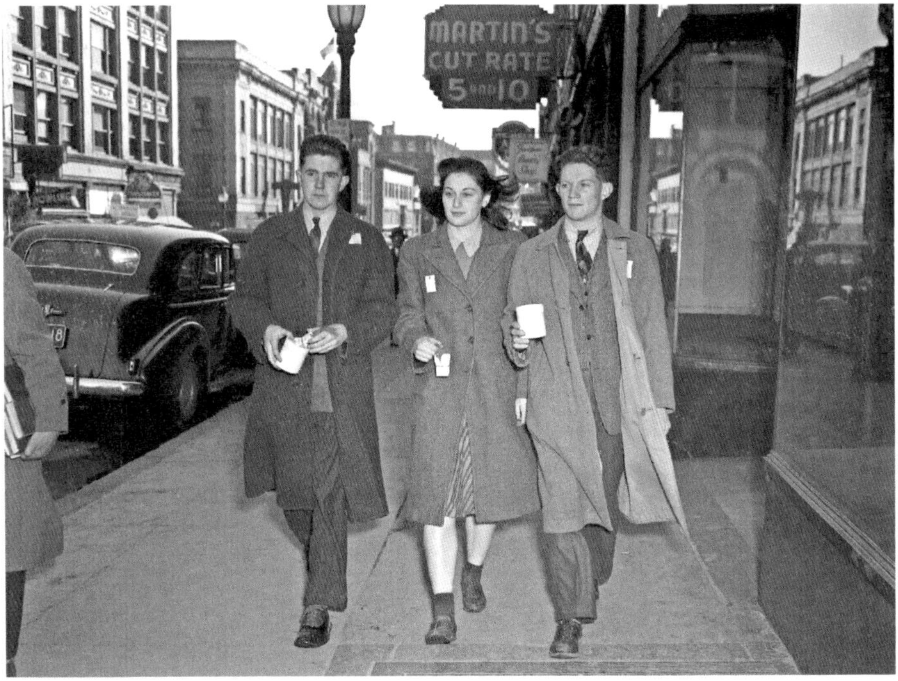

"Soliciting Donations." Several tag days were held to raise money for the widows and children of the fallen firefighters, March 15, 1941. *Bauman Collection, Stonehill College.*

unanimously not to charge injured firemen for services rendered by the hospital. Another touching tribute was made by one of the firemen. The *Brockton Enterprise* reported that when firemen were paid on Tuesday, Albert Grady endorsed his "check and handed it to the captain with a simple 'for the fund Capt.'"[44]

The *Brockton Enterprise* reported one of the more unusual donations to be that of $50, received from famed movie star James Cagney. The star, who had a summer home on Martha's Vineyard, sent the donation as "a friend of the late Chief Daley in his memory." William F. Daley was promoted to Brockton fire chief in 1916 and served until 1928, when he drowned on May 14, along with several prominent Brocktonians at Moosehead Lake in Maine. Fire Chief Dickinson was named his successor.

Saturday, March 15, 1941, was a banner day for the fund, with several activities contributing. The fund itself sponsored a tag day in which volunteers throughout the city solicited donations and each contributor received a "tag" for their donation. Over $3,000.00 was raised. That same day, the Salvation Army organized a Doughnut Day. Under the direction of Adjutant Albert J. Warren and Adjutant William Bovill, two Salvation Army trucks were stationed on Main Street, and "Lassies" in Salvation Army uniforms carried baskets of doughnuts in cellophane bags marked "Firemen's Relief Fund." The doughnuts were sold for whatever the donor wanted to give, and a total of $28.49 was raised. The doughnuts were donated by various Brockton bakeries and were similar to what was distributed the night of the Strand Theatre fire. The two crews in charge of the sale were the same Salvation Army crews that reported to every fire in the city, dispensing coffee and doughnuts.[45]

Monday, March 17, 1941, the other five theaters in Brockton held benefit shows to raise monies for the fund. An evening show was held at the Brockton Theatre, on Main Street, which comprised twenty vaudeville acts, including the Dornan Brothers and Mary, a professional act from Brockton. Other acts included the Vega Quartette, winners of the Plymouth County quartette contest; Jimmy Lawton, impersonator; and Richard Roclevich, tiny cornetist. Art Kendrew provided music for the show, and musicians from the Brockton

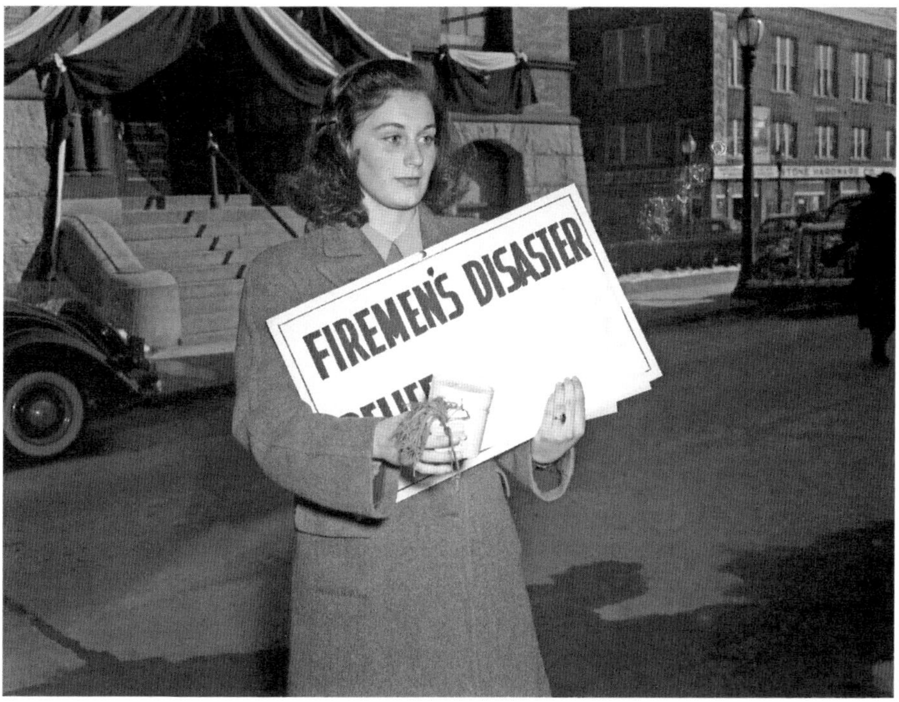

A Brockton teenager collects for the Firemen's Disaster Fund during the tag day held on Saturday, March 15, 1941. *Bauman Collection, Stonehill College.*

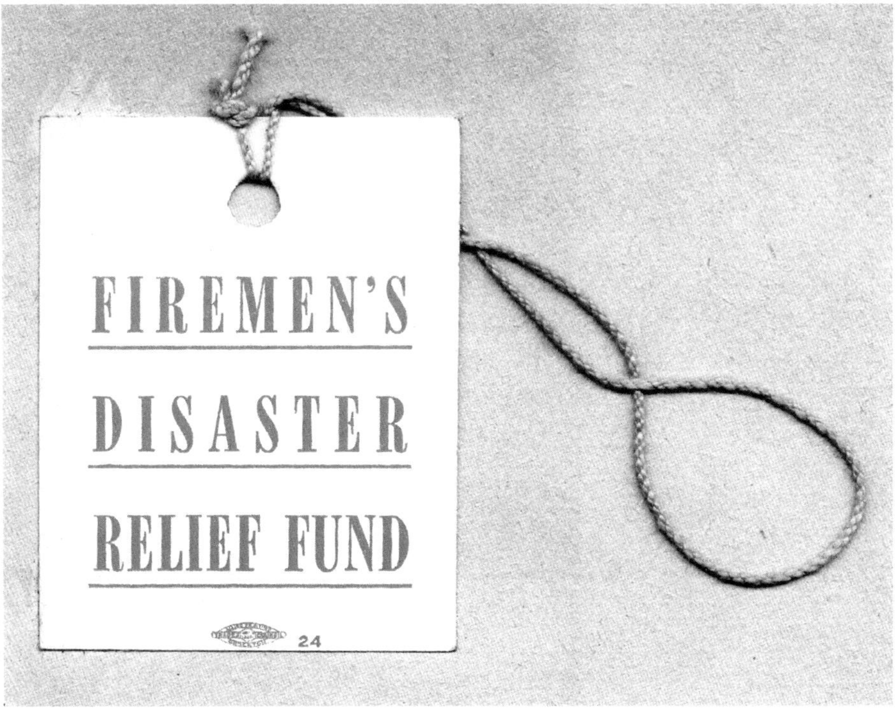

Those donating to the Firemen's Disaster Relief Fund on tag day received this tag. *Bauman Collection, Stonehill College.*

Musicians Union and the Brockton Legion Band played outside the Brockton Theatre from 7:30 to 8:30 p.m. The Colonial, Modern, Park and Keith Theatres presented special feature pictures and short subjects from 11:00 p.m. to 1:00 a.m.

Also, on March 17, 1941, a group of Legionnaires traveled to the New England amateur boxing champions' bouts at the Boston Garden at the invitation of Gene Driscoll, chairman of the boxing committee of the New England Association of the AAU (American Athletic Union). A total of $441 was collected under the direction of John S. Mara, commander of the American Legion, Brockton Post. The collection was made possible because the state boxing commission voted to waive its rule against collections at boxing matches. Boxing matches were also chosen as the venue for the Jewish War Veterans to raise money for the fund. Staging benefit boxing bouts at Massasoit Hall in Brockton on Friday, March 21, 1941, the group raised several hundred dollars for the fund.

For some cities, it was a chance to the return the kindness once shown to them by the City of Brockton. In 1930, Nashua, New Hampshire, suffered a disastrous fire that destroyed several factories and left more than 1,500 people homeless. Brockton assisted Nashua's rehabilitation by donating cash and shoes. Nashua, "Paying It Forward" to the City of Brockton, contributed a donation of over $1,086 from tag day collections and $200 from its own Firemen's Relief Association to the relief fund. Nashua mayor Eugene H. Lemay and Nashua Fire Chief Anthony J. Malloy presented the check to Mayor Rowe on Friday, March 21, 1941. A photograph of the check being presented was taken by photographer Stanley Bauman and included Fire Chief Frank F. Dickinson, Firemen's Relief Committee chairman Edward A. Dinneen, Mayor Rowe, Mayor Lemay, Chief Malloy and Lieutenant James A. Brahaley of the Nashua Fire Department. Other cities and towns that personally presented checks included Lynn, Massachusetts ($514) and East Bridgewater, Massachusetts ($431). Herbert E. Macauley, mayor of Newport, Rhode Island, presented a check for $1,538 collected from Newport residents and from men in the Newport Naval Torpedo Station. The city had to request special permission from the secretary of the navy to enter the base to perform the collection.[46]

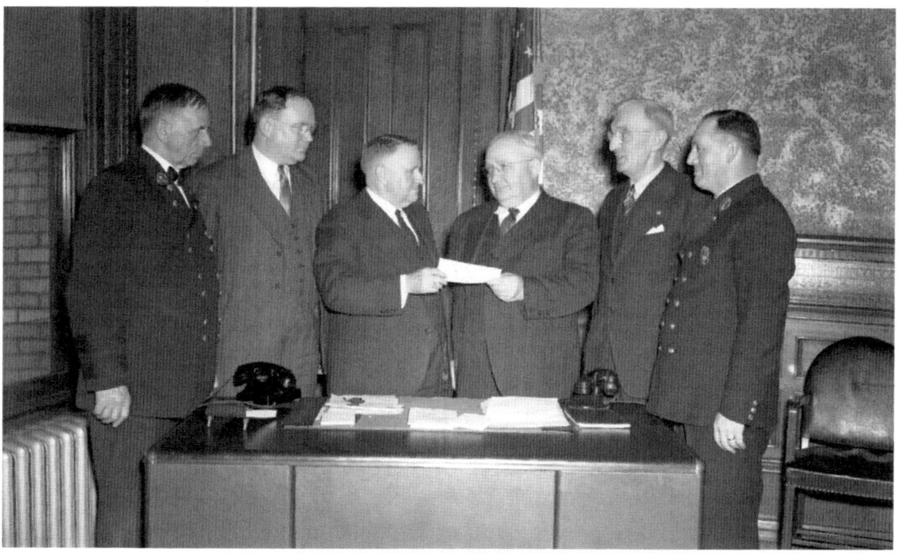

"Paying It Forward." In 1930, Nashua, New Hampshire, suffered a disastrous fire that destroyed several factories and left more than 1,500 people homeless. Brockton assisted Nashua's rehabilitation by donating cash and shoes. Here the City of Nashua "pays it forward" and presents a check to Brockton mayor Rowe. Pictured are Fire Chief Frank F. Dickinson, Firemen's Relief Committee chairman Edward A. Dinneen, Mayor Rowe, Nashua mayor Eugene H. Lemay, Chief Anthony J. Malloy and Lieutenant James A. Brahaley of the Nashua Fire Department. *Bauman Collection, Stonehill College.*

One of the largest single donations came from the State of Rhode Island, which held its own fund drive, raising nearly $7,000. In a ceremony held in the ballroom of the Rhode Island State House, Governor J. Howard McGrath presented the check to fund chairman Dinneen. In total, the state gave almost $10,000 when including checks presented separately by cities, including aforementioned Newport as well as Pawtucket ($117).

Within a year of the fire, as the city planned to commemorate the first anniversary, the *Brockton Enterprise* reported $125,000 had been raised to help the families of the dead firemen and those injured in the fire. In March 1941, the *Brockton Enterprise* reported that the disposition of the fund would be overseen by a committee of trustees and would take place over a period of years according to the needs of the families. The trustees included Albert Doyle, director of Brockton National Bank, chairman; William G. Allan, treasurer of Brockton Savings Bank, treasurer; Harry K. Stone, clerk; Mayor Rowe; Dr. George A. Buckley; William T. Card, chairman of assessors; Fire Chief Dickinson, Judge Maurice J. Murphy; attorney Clarence C. Reed, attorney Eben G. Townes; and fund chairman Edward A. Dinneen. However, with the exception of the listing of donations reported by the *Brockton Enterprise*, no official accounting of donations or distributions of the fund has been found.

RELIEF ASSOCIATION PAYMENTS AND ANNUITIES

Within twenty-four hours after the fire, the Brockton Firemen's Relief Association paid a total of $6,000 to the families of the deceased firemen, each receiving a one-time payment of $500. An additional $120 was paid for flowers. The association also pledged to expend money for a bronze marker over each firefighter's grave. The Brockton Firemen's Relief Association paid injured firefighters $7 a week, as specified in the organization's bylaws.[47] A 1956 copy of the Brockton Firemen's Relief Association Bylaws stated that "payment would be made to any member...who is unable to perform his duties...until he is able to report for duty...it being provided, however, that benefits shall not be paid for a period longer than six months, and no such benefit shall be paid unless such a disability shall result in the loss of pay." It is unknown if this exact time frame was in place at the time of the Strand Theatre or, if it was, if the stipulation was suspended for those who were out longer than the six months. The $7 per week would have been about one-fifth of a fireman's normal weekly wage. The state's Permanent Fireman's Association paid each deceased fireman's family a one-time $1,000 death benefit.

The City of Brockton also assisted the families with annuities to the fire widows. On Monday, March 17, 1941, one week after the fire, the city council passed an order granting annuities to the thirteen widows and the fifteen children who were under the age of eighteen in the amounts of $1,000 and $200, respectively. The order passed as follows:

> *Whereas, there has been filed with the city treasurer, a certificate by a board of physicians appointed in accordance with chapter 32, section 39, of the general laws that the following members of the city of Brockton Captain John F. Carroll, Lieutenant Raymond A. Mitchell, George A. Collins, Bartholomew Herlihy, Frederick Kelly, Martin E. Lipper, Matthew E. McGeary, Ray A. McKeraghan, John M. McNeill, Denis P. Murphy, William J. Murphy, Daniel C. O'Brien, and Henry E. Sullivan lost their lives while in the performance of their duties at a fire in the Strand Theatre on March 10, 1941 therefore be it ordered that annuities...be paid dating from March 11, 1941 to each widow for herself as long as she remains unmarried and for each child of such deceased firemen while such child is under 18 years of age...and be it further ordered, that such amounts be paid semimonthly the same to be paid from the pension account.*

At the same city council meeting, Councilman Joseph H. Downey requested the restoration of the final 7½ percent of the 15 percent wage cut imposed on the entire fire department in 1932. The measure was approved at the council's March 24, 1941, meeting.[48] In 1941, the average firefighter's salary was $1,800 to $2,300 per year depending on his rank. Firefighters worked an average of eighty-four hours per week.

TRIBUTES

In addition to the Firemen's Disaster Relief Committee Fund, tributes were paid to the fallen. On Tuesday, March 11, 1941, the *Brockton Enterprise* ran a cartoon by Brockton cartoonist Weston Jenney titled "For I Am the Way and the Life." Jenney, who died in 1965, frequently published cartoons in the *Brockton Enterprise*, including one on Wednesday, March 15, 1951, titled

"Carrying On," featuring a drawing of the Squad A engine surrounded by city and fund officials.[49] Yet none of his cartoons has had the effect of "For I Am the Way and the Life," a copy of which is on permanent display at the Brockton Fire Museum.

Several of Brockton's stores created special window displays to pay tribute to the fallen firefighters. Fraser's Department Store created a unique window as a way to solicit support for the Firemen's Relief Fund. Against a backdrop of deep purple, an open wax hand held bills of various denominations with coins scattered about surrounded by tag-day coin boxes. The open hand was to signify "free giving."

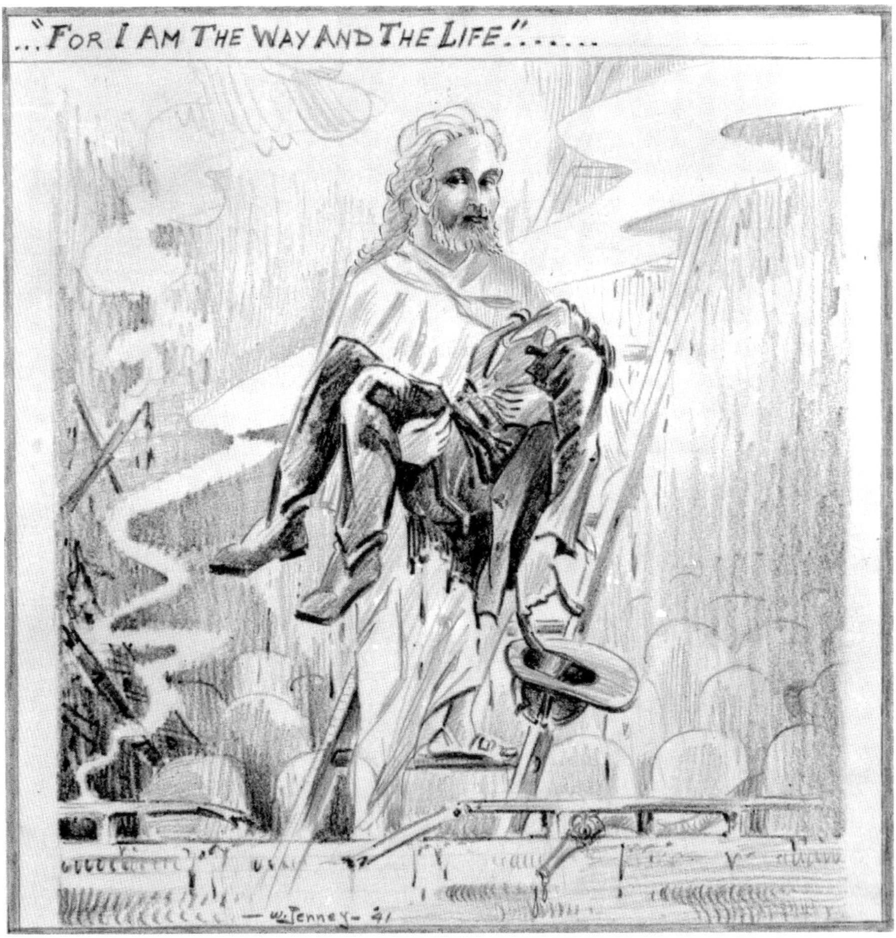

A memorial cartoon, "For I Am the Way and the Life," was illustrated by Brockton cartoonist Wes Jenney. *Brockton Fire Museum.*

Other windows were more poignant. Edgar's Department store featured a window with firemen's helmets and axes surrounded by flowers with a wreath in the middle in memoriam. The inscription in the window read, "We pause to extend our deepest sympathies to the families of Brockton's heroic firemen." The Storey & Company's window included plants on each side of a wreath in the center. On each side of the wreath was an American flag. The Edison Company window showcased a picture of firemen and children with a wreath in the center, along with a basket of flowers. The front window case of the Bessie Baker's Company at 58 Main Street paid tribute to the fallen with a fireman's hat in front of a placard bearing the inscription "Brave men, living and dead," a quote from Abraham Lincoln. Its rear window contained a large bouquet of white flowers. The P&Q Clothing Company at 123 Main Street paid tribute simply by emptying its window while the Loring Studio, also on Main Street, placed a wreath in its window.

Yet only the photo of one of the windows has been found. Taken by Stanley Bauman and printed in the *Brockton Enterprise* is the window created by Kennedy's Department Store. Located adjacent to the Strand and whose roof had been used as a platform to fight the fire, Kennedy's created a display featuring the helmets of three firemen—a captain, a lieutenant and a private—representing the ranks of the men who died. Colored lights shone down on the helmets, which were flanked by ferns. Underneath the helmets were two sentences of a quote by Homer: "But sure the eye of time beholds no name. So blest as thine in all the rolls of fame." Today, a replica of that display can be found at the Brockton Fire Museum as part of its exhibit on the Strand fire.[50]

On Sunday, March 16, 1941, the South Congregational Church in its parish calendar paid tribute to the thirteen deceased firemen with the following quote from John Bunyan's *The Pilgrim's Progress*: "So they passed over, and all the trumpets sounded for them on the other side."[51] The church also raised $100 for the fund. Other churches also held tributes. St. Edward's Catholic Church, which ended a two-week mission on Sunday, March 16, 1941, paid tribute to the fallen firemen, with a special remembrance of the members of the church who at the time of the tragedy were making the mission. McKeraghan, O'Brien, Sullivan, McGeary and McNeill were all members of the church. Only Sullivan is mentioned by name as making the mission, which started for the men on Sunday, March 9, 1941.

On Monday, March 24, 1941, the Brockton City Council unanimously passed a resolution to pay tribute to the men who lost their lives and offer

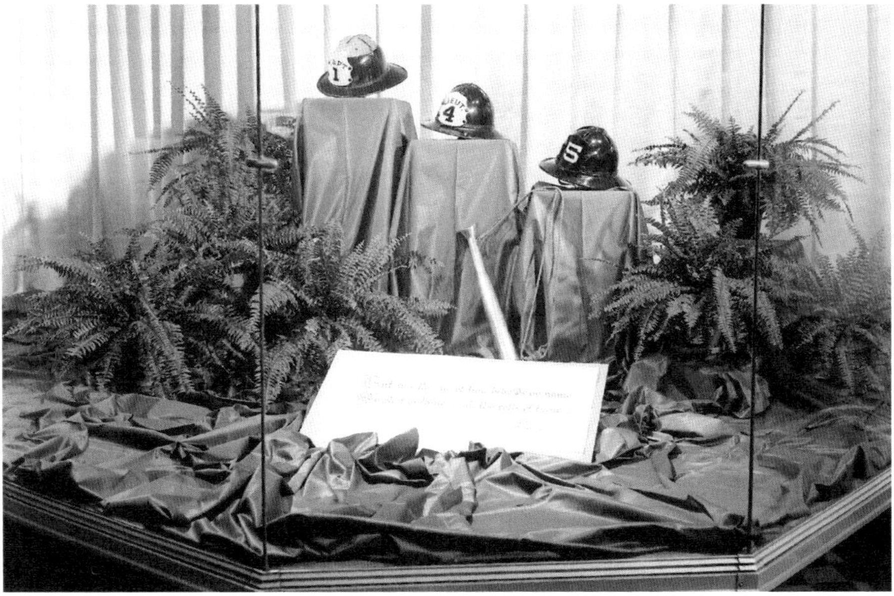

This window display at Kennedy's Department Store, located next to the theater, paid tribute to departed firefighters. It was one of several done by various Brockton Main Street businesses. *Bauman Collection, Stonehill College.*

sympathy to the families. A copy of the resolution was sent to each family. Other resolutions of sympathy were received from the Rhode Island General Assembly, Cambridge (Massachusetts) City Council and Randolph (Massachusetts) Chamber of Commerce.

On Tuesday, April 8, 1941, a delegation from New York came to Brockton to present a donation to the fund. However, in planning the trip, it requested that a memorial Mass be held:

> *The New York group was headed by Vincent J. Jane, president of the New York City Firemen's Benevolent Association and first vice president of the International Association of Firefighters. It also included a representative from the New York State Fireman's Association, the chiefs of New York City, along with the captains, lieutenants and privates which made up the executive board of the New York City relief association. Arrangements were taken care of by Captain Charles G. McCarthy, president of the Barry Fire Club, Local 144, International Association of Firefighters, which was organized in 1920 and named in memory of Edward J. Barry a former fireman at the Central Station who was a diligent worker for the cause of firefighters.*[52]

Whereas, God in His Infinite Wisdom has called to Him thirteen members of the Brockton Fire Department, and

Whereas, These heroic men, in serving the people at the Strand Theatre Fire on March 10, 1941, made the supreme sacrifice; therefore be it

Resolved, That the City Council of the City of Brockton, in behalf of all citizens, humbly pays tribute to this gallant corps of men who, representing all that is brave and noble in mankind, offered up their lives in the protection and defense of their fellow men; and be it further

Resolved, That the names of these loyal men,

CAPTAIN JOHN F. CARROLL
LIEUTENANT RAYMOND A. MITCHELL
GEORGE A. COLLINS
BARTHOLOMEW HERLIHY
FREDERICK F. KELLEY
MARTIN E. LIPPER
MATTHEW E. McGEARY
ROY A. McKERAGHAN
JOHN M. McNEILL
DENIS P. MURPHY
WILLIAM J. MURPHY
DANIEL C. O'BRIEN
HENRY E. SULLIVAN

already enshrined in the hearts of our citizenry, be inscribed upon a plaque of enduring form, and be it finally

Resolved, That to the families of these heroes there be extended our heartfelt sympathy; That these resolutions be spread upon our records; and That a copy of the same be sent to the bereaved families.

By the special committee on resolutions,
COUNCILLOR WARREN S. KEITH, Chairman
COUNCILLOR ALBERT G. SMITH
COUNCILLOR ROBERT E. NASH

IN CITY COUNCIL, MARCH 24, 1941
Unanimously adopted by a rising vote.

J. ALBERT SULLIVAN, Clerk.

Approved:
FRED D. ROWE, Mayor.
March 29, 1941.

A true copy, Attest:

J. Albert Sullivan
City Clerk.

On March 24, 1941, the Brockton City Council passed this resolution, which paid tribute to the thirteen fallen firefighters. *Brockton Fire Museum.*

Held at St. Patrick's Church in Brockton, the spiritual tribute drew over one thousand people, including delegations of firefighters from across New England. After the service, the New York firemen presented checks for over $5,700 to the fund, helping to bring the total to over $100,000.[53]

On Sunday, June 23, 1941, the Brockton Firemen's Relief Association held its annual memorial service for deceased members of the department.

It was held at Porter Congregational Church, and Reverend Horace F. Holton, DD, delivered the sermon, which included a tribute to those who lost their lives at the Strand:

> *In the line of duty, that is the fireman's code, and it is his religion. It was the code of all these whom we are here this evening to honor. In the line of duty they submitted to the discipline of their calling, they endured the monotony of its routine and faced its recurring dangers; doing well and quickly each duty as it came.... They have lived as they died in the line of duty.*

The service was preceded by a street parade of firemen, city officials and Legionnaires (including the Legionnaire Band), who assembled in front of the Central Fire Station, paraded west on Pleasant Street to Warren Avenue, south on Warren Avenue to Legion Parkway, east on Legion Parkway to Main Street and north on Main Street to the Porter Congregational Church. Upon arriving at the church, the band played several numbers as paraders entered the church. Also in attendance were the families of the Strand fire victims and other deceased firemen. Firemen William Kelleher and Jeremiah Sheehan, still recovering from wounds suffered at the Strand and unable to parade, also attended.

ANNIVERSARIES AND MEMORIALS

Within nine months of the Strand Theatre fire, Japan attacked Pearl Harbor, and the United States entered World War II. As the first anniversary approached, focus was on the war in Europe and the Pacific. Headlines fixated totally on war news, with local news relegated to the inside pages. On Tuesday, March 10, 1942, page nine of the *Brockton Enterprise* featured Wes Jenney's cartoon "For I Am the Way and the Life," along with a short article looking back on the fire and information on the memorial service to be held that night at Brockton City Hall. The following day, page eleven of the second section featured a photo from the service about the unveiling of a tablet inscribed with the names of the thirteen Strand victims.

The tablet is a piece of coal (anthracite) carved by William J. Owens, then a fireman with the Scranton, Pennsylvania Fire Department. It was presented by Scranton Firefighters, then Local 669, to Brockton Firefighters Local 144 on August 1, 1941. Captain Charles G. McCarthy,

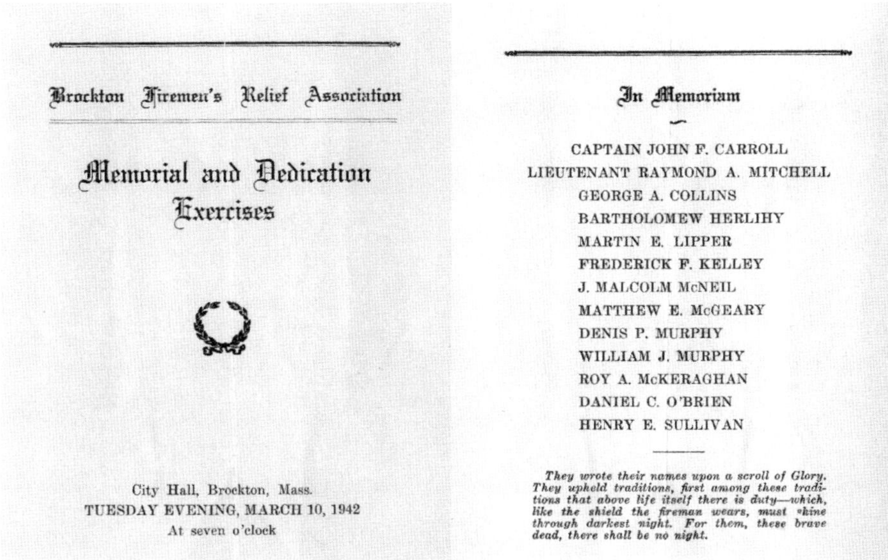
Brockton Firemen's Relief Association

Memorial and Dedication Exercises

City Hall, Brockton, Mass.
TUESDAY EVENING, MARCH 10, 1942
At seven o'clock

In Memoriam

CAPTAIN JOHN F. CARROLL
LIEUTENANT RAYMOND A. MITCHELL
GEORGE A. COLLINS
BARTHOLOMEW HERLIHY
MARTIN E. LIPPER
FREDERICK F. KELLEY
J. MALCOLM McNEIL
MATTHEW E. McGEARY
DENIS P. MURPHY
WILLIAM J. MURPHY
ROY A. McKERAGHAN
DANIEL C. O'BRIEN
HENRY E. SULLIVAN

They wrote their names upon a scroll of Glory. They upheld traditions, first among these traditions that above life itself there is duty—which, like the shield the fireman wears, must shine through darkest night. For them, these brave dead, there shall be no night.

This first anniversary program, dated March 10, 1942, was saved and found in a scrapbook created by Phyllis E. Peck about the fire. *Brockton Fire Museum.*

president of Local 144, presented the tablet to Mayor Joseph H. Downey at the ceremony held March 10, 1942. The mayor accepted the memorial tablet on behalf of the city and its citizens. Enclosed in glass, the engraved piece of coal sits on a marble base. The base is engraved with the names of other Brockton firefighters who lost their lives in the line of duty. Also present at the dedication were the widows and families of the deceased firemen.[54]

Every year on March 10, since 1942, the first anniversary of the fire, Brockton firefighters have held a service in the rotunda of Brockton City Hall and paid tribute to their fallen comrades who responded to the Strand Theatre but never returned. As years passed, the memorial was moved from the rotunda to the corridor of city hall in front of the City Clerk's Office. In later years, it was returned to its original location in the rotunda. At some point, a marble tablet with the names of the deceased firefighters was also placed on the wall of the rotunda among other tablets bearing the names of those from Brockton who died serving their country in combat.

New firefighters joined the ranks and honored the fallen, including the sons of Strand victims Lieutenant Raymond A. Mitchell and firefighter Roy McKeraghan. Others who fought at the Strand rose through the

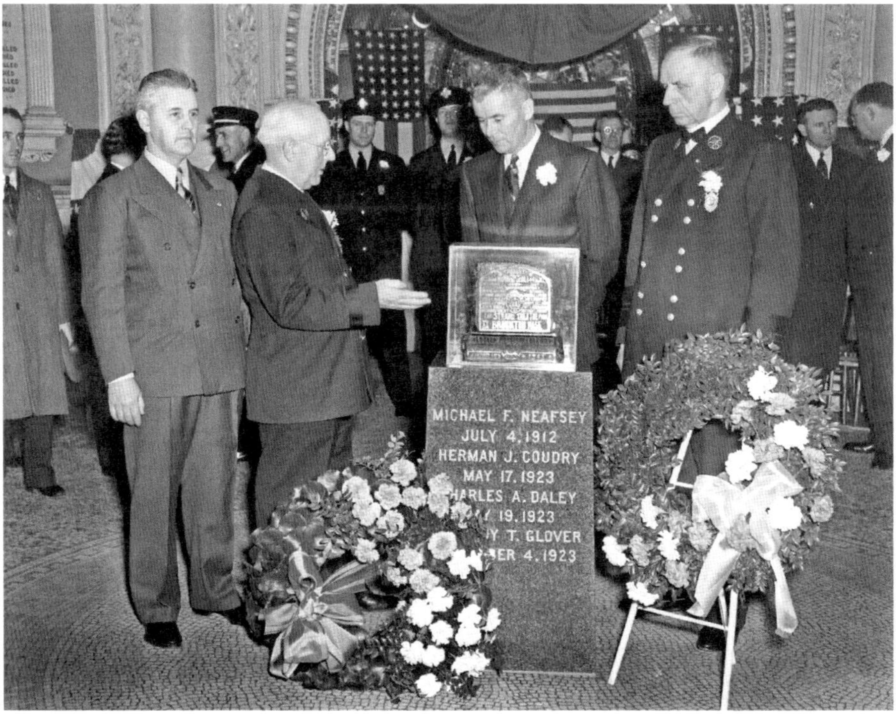

On March 10, 1942, the first anniversary of the fire, a coal memorial was donated by Scranton, Pennsylvania firefighters, then Local 669, was unveiled. The anthracite was carved in August 1941 by Scranton firefighter William J. Owens. *Brockton Fire Museum.*

ranks, including Deputy Chief Lynch, who was appointed chief of the department in 1947 after Chief Dickinson retired in 1946. Edward Burrell, a rookie with two years' experience the night of the fire, was appointed chief of the department on October 29, 1963. A photo from the twenty-sixth-anniversary memorial on March 10, 1967, pictured Fire Chief Edward L. Burrell; Clayton S. and Raymond A. Mitchell, sons of fallen firefighter Lieutenant Raymond A. Mitchell; Richard J. McKeraghan, son of fallen firefighter Roy A. McKeraghan; Reverend James H. O'Brien Jr., fire department Protestant chaplain; Reverend James L. Breau, fire department Catholic chaplain; Mayor Alvin Jack Sims; and Harry W. Olson, Brockton Public Safety Commission member.

Thus, each year, they came, honored and remembered, and each year, photographer Stanley A. Bauman photographed the wreath being placed at the memorial's base. Some years, the photos were accompanied by a larger article and even pictures taken by Bauman the night of the fire.

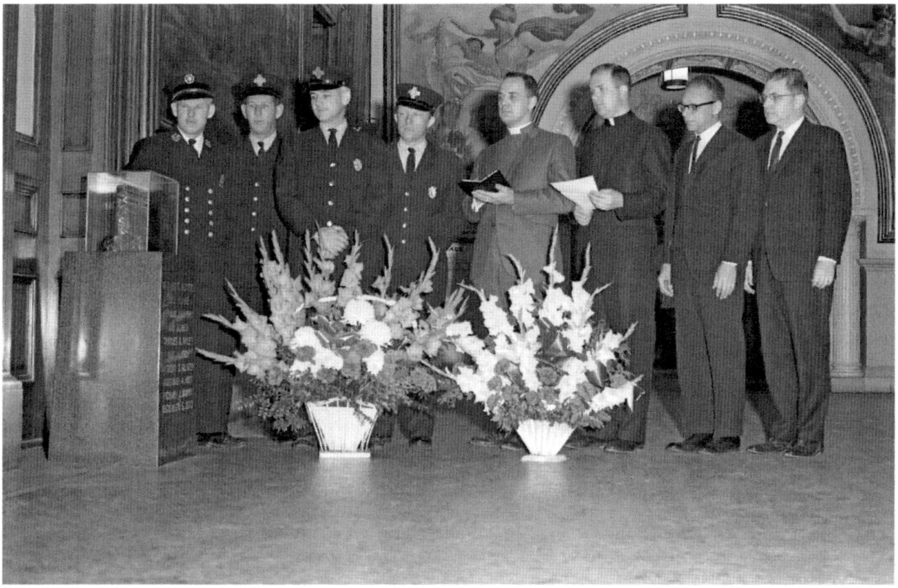

This photo was taken at the twenty-sixth-anniversary memorial on March 10, 1967, and features Fire Chief Edward L. Burrell; Clayton S. and Raymond A. Mitchell, sons of fallen firefighter Lieutenant Raymond A. Mitchell; Richard J. McKeraghan, son of fallen firefighter Roy A. McKeraghan; Reverend James H. O'Brien Jr., fire department Protestant chaplain; Reverend James L. Breau, fire department Catholic chaplain; Mayor Alvin Jack Sims; and Harry W. Olson, Brockton Public Safety Commission member. *Bauman Collection, Stonehill College.*

Anniversaries such as the tenth, twentieth and twenty-fifth even warranted publication on the front page. But for more than sixty-five years, the coal tablet stood as one of the only memorials to the fire tragedy. It is speculated that the country's involvement in World War II left little time or money for a permanent memorial. At the end of World War II, the Strand tragedy was a memory, as the country moved forward and worked to honor the hundreds killed and wounded serving overseas in the war. Yet Brockton firefighters never forgot, and in 2001, sixty years after the fire, talk turned to a more permanent memorial. One reason for the renewed call was described by Lieutenant Richard Baker during an interview in March 2002: "September 11th changed everything and makes it more important to remember fallen firefighters."[55]

The committee eventually raised around $150,000 for the memorial. Funds were raised through raffles, motorcycle runs, potluck dinners and other events. Generous donations were also received from several organizations and individuals, including but not limited to Bay State Gas

Company (now Columbia Gas), DeZine Land Construction, Whitman Post No. 697, National Grid, *Brockton Enterprise*, Brockton Hospital, the Rotary Club of Brockton, HarborOne Credit Union (now HarborOne Bank), Crescent Credit Union, Conley Funeral Home and the Plahn, Carroll, Murphy and Woodward families.

There were several proposals for the memorial, including a fireman sitting with head bowed surrounded by thirteen helmets and one incorporating theater seats. Ultimately, a simple ten-and-a-half-foot bronze-and-granite statue of a Brockton firefighter in a uniform representative of those worn in the 1940s, kneeling and head bowed, was chosen. A firefighter's helmet sits at the firefighter's feet with the number 13 to represent the thirteen fallen firefighters. The statue's face is modeled after Edward "Sonny" Burrell, the last surviving member of the Brockton fire department who responded to the fire. The base of the statue includes the names of the deceased firemen on the front and the Fireman's Prayer on the back of the statue.

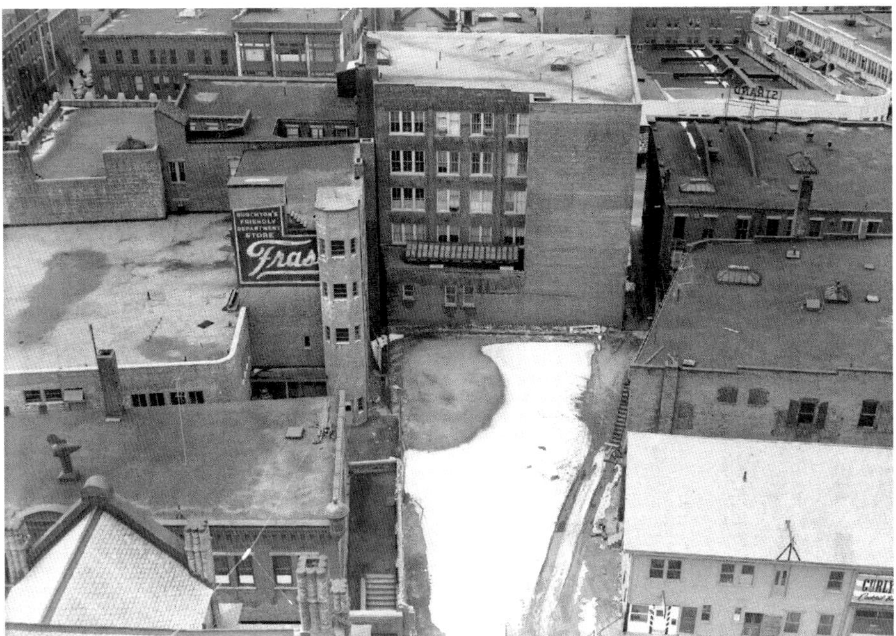

The site of the Strand Theatre taken eleven years after the fire shows the oddly shaped vacant lot where the Strand Theatre once stood and how the surrounding buildings made fighting the fire difficult, March 10, 1952. *Bauman Collection, Stonehill College.*

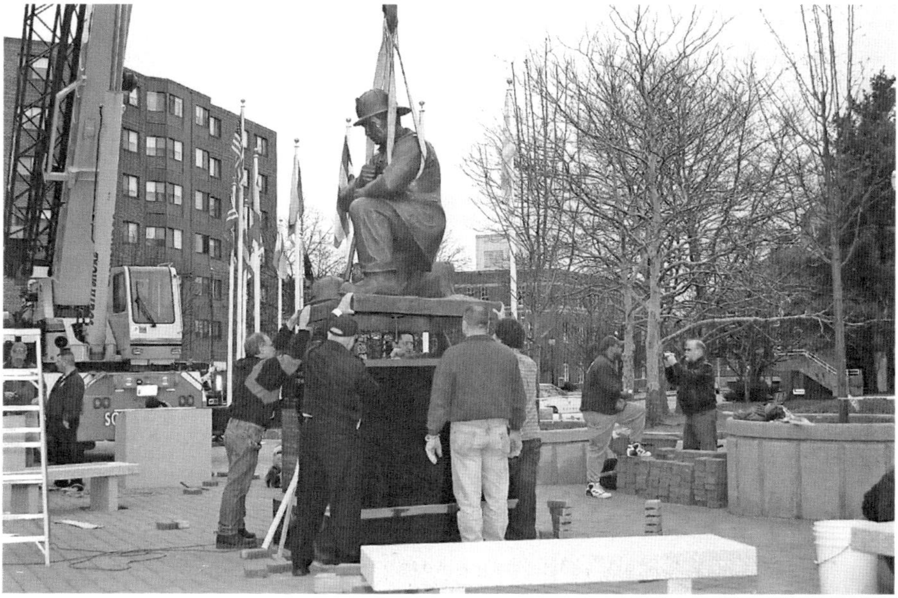

Workers from Skylight Studios in Woburn, Massachusetts, along with volunteers from the fire department, including then Fire Chief Kenneth Galligan, position the Strand memorial statue in its permanent spot at City Hall Plaza, March 2008. *Bob Myers, 105 Fire Photos.*

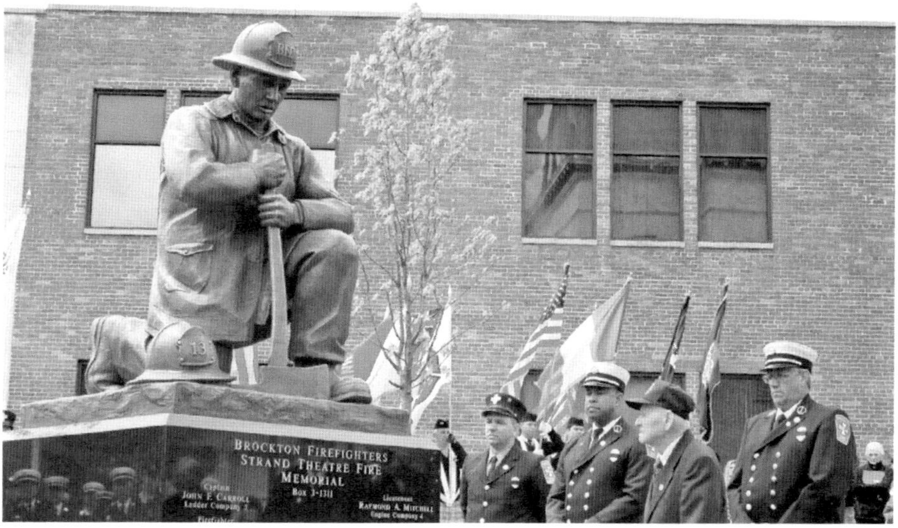

Retired Brockton fire chief and Strand Theatre fire survivor Edward "Sonny" Burrell attended the dedication of the Strand Theatre memorial at City Hall Plaza, March 10, 2008. *Bob Myers, 105 Fire Photos.*

A Fireman's Prayer

When I am called to duty God,
Wherever flames may rage,
Give me strength to save some life
Whatever be its age

Help me embrace a little child
Before it is too late
Or save an older person from
The horror of that fate.

Enable me to be alert
And hear the weakest shout
And quickly and efficiently
To put the fire out.

I want to fill my calling and
To give the best in me
To guard my every neighbor and
Protect his property

And if according to my fate
I am to lose my life
Please bless with your protecting hand
My children and my wife.

The memorial is located in City Hall Plaza in the shadow of the empty lot where the Strand Theatre once stood. Local lore states that after the fire, the city council vowed that no other future theater in the city would be named Strand. The statue was sculpted by Robert Shure of Skylight Studios in Woburn, Massachusetts, for a cost of $136,000. It was erected in March 2008. Site work was provided by Brockton firefighters. Retired Fire Chief Burrell helped unveil the statue, formally dedicated on May 10, 2008, and remarked, "I never thought I'd live long enough to see it."[56] Chief Burell died six years later at the age of ninety-nine, on January 15, 2014. According to retired Fire Chief Kenneth F. Galligan, who was Brockton's fire chief when the memorial was built and dedicated, the memorial is a reminder to all of the dedication of firefighters who serve and protect life and property, as well as a reminder of the dangers firefighters face in the performance of their duties.[57]

6
Epilogue

Organized by an act of legislature on March, 1, 1846, the Brockton Fire Department celebrated its 170th anniversary in 2016. The year also marked the 75th anniversary of the Strand Theatre fire. During the annual remembrance held at the memorial in City Hall Plaza, sponsored by Brockton Firefighters Local 144, Archibald Gormley Jr., president of Local 144, presented members of each victim's family a commemorative coin in an acrylic frame with the deceased firefighter's name engraved on the case. He was joined by Brockton Fire Chief Michael Williams and Professional Fire Fighters of Massachusetts (PFFM) president Edward A. Kelly and International Association of Fire Fighters (IAFF) Third District vice-president Jay Colbert. Firefighter William Hill, treasurer of Local 144, announced the names of each fallen firefighter. The IAFF presented families with the IAFF Medal of Valor medallion, and wreaths were placed at the coal memorial still located in the rotunda of Brockton City Hall.

At least twenty Brockton firefighters have given their lives in the line of duty, thirteen at the Strand. The Strand fire caused immediate changes to how the Brockton Fire Department fought fires. In addition to the rule stipulating no rubber gloves were to be used when fighting fires (a rule that still exists today), the fear of a building collapse caused Chief Dickinson to be more cautious in how the department fought fires after the Strand. This was illustrated in two large fires that happened within two years of the Strand fire. The first fire, at the Palace Hotel, located at Main and High (now Frederick Douglass Avenue) Streets in the Metropolitan Block, occurred on

April 6, 1941, less than a month after the Strand fire. Fire Alarm Box 1311 was once again sounded to alert the fire department. Arriving at the scene, firefighters immediately went inside the building to rescue occupants of the hotel. Upon his arrival, Chief Dickinson "ordered all firemen to keep out of the building," declaring, "This entire building isn't worth the price of one fireman."[58] Even once crews were allowed into the building, caution was given to "watch the wall." A year and a half later, on December 30, 1942, a general alarm fire at the five-story brick building formerly home to the Stacy-Adams Shoe Factory, located on Montello Street near Centre Street, threatened an entire city block. Still mindful of the Strand, Dickinson ordered all men from the building as soon as it appeared the walls were weak, and from then on, the fire was fought from the outside.[59]

Today, advances in firefighting have helped make situations like the Strand less likely. In 1941, firefighters operated with minimal equipment, and essential firefighting tools that are relatively common in today's fire departments were lacking. Firefighters at the Strand did not have radios, full bunker gear or SCBA (self-contained-breathing-apparatus). In the words of retired Brockton Fire Chief Edward L. Burrell, appointed to the department in 1939, "All they gave us was a helmet." As a result of having no radios, there was no way for firefighters outside the theater to immediately communicate with those inside that the fire had broken through to the outside, and those firefighters inside did not realize the severity of the conflagration or how extensively it had spread. Since the Strand Theatre fire, experts say one of the biggest advances made in firefighting and firefighter safety is equipping every firefighter with a portable radio.[60] Brockton received its first portable radios on October 20, 1973.[61] Today, in addition to the introduction of radios, the formal incident command system provides the officer in charge a formal fireground system and tactics to enhance fireground extinguishing operations and firefighter safety. In 2008, Casey Grant, program director of the National Fire Protection Association, stated in an interview with the *Brockton Enterprise* that "communication is a very important factor....Then you just didn't know where people were."[62]

Retired Brockton Fire Chief Kenneth Galligan believes that firefighters today are better trained in both fighting structure fires and knowing how buildings are constructed. Additional equipment advances include alarms worn by firefighters that sound if a firefighter goes down, as well as thermal imaging cameras that enable firefighters to detect heat and fire in walls or ceilings. On-scene paramedics and Rapid Intervention teams have also improved firefighter safety at the scene. Building sprinklers and smoke

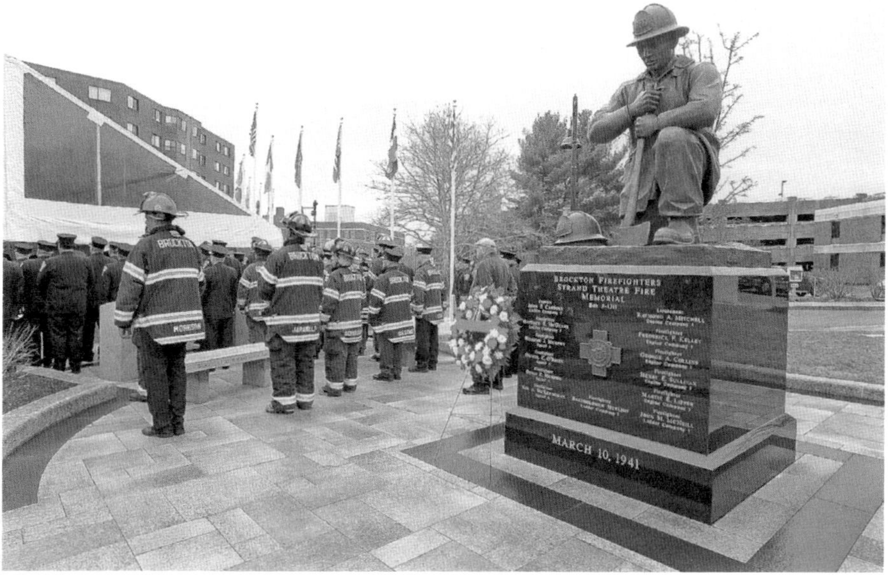

Firefighters stand at attention in front of the Strand Theatre memorial at City Hall Plaza during the seventy-fifth anniversary memorial service, March 10, 2016. *Bob Myers, 105 Fire Photos.*

detector alarms have greatly improved the safety of building occupants and responding firefighters.

But even with the advances in technology, it still takes a special person to "run towards the fire and danger as others flee." In the words of Edward F. Croker, chief of the New York Fire Department from 1899 to 1911:

> *I have no ambition in this world but one, and that is to be a fireman. The position may, in the eyes of some, appear to be a lowly one; but those who know the work which a fireman has to do, believes it is a noble calling. Our proudest moment is to save lives. Under the impulse of such thoughts the nobility of the occupation thrills us and stimulates us to deeds of daring, even of supreme sacrifice.*

Notes

Chapter 2

1. "New Strand Very Handsome," *Brockton Daily Enterprise*, 1.
2. Ibid.
3. Wilmeth with Miller, *Cambridge Guide to American Theatre.*
4. "Strand Theatre a Great House," *Brockton Daily Enterprise.*
5. "Strand Open, Invite Public," *Brockton Daily Enterprise.*

Chapter 3

6. Pitcher, "Remembering the Strand Theatre."
7. Lyons, "Enterprise Man Aids in Rescue."
8. LaLiberte, "Strand Disaster," 4.
9. "Eyewitness Accounts Are Given by Sad Firemen," *Brockton Daily Enterprise.*
10. LaLiberte, "Strand Disaster," 1.
11. "Eyewitness Accounts Are Given by Sad Firemen," *Brockton Daily Enterprise.*
12. Peck, Strand scrapbook, 67.
13. Ibid., 18.
14. Ibid., 67.
15. Ibid., 7.
16. "Volunteer to Aid Rescuers," *Brockton Daily Enterprise.*

17. Mary Alice LaLiberte Bruce in discussion with Nicole Casper, August 2016.
18. LaLiberte, "Strand Disaster," 5.
19. Peck, Strand scrapbook, 67.
20. Ibid.
21. "Doctors and Nurses Rise to the Occasion," *Brockton Daily Enterprise.*
22. Peck, Strand scrapbook, 59.
23. Desk Journal Station Six, Brockton Fire Department, March 11, 1941.
24. "'Bart' Herlihy, 13th Fire Victim Is Laid at Rest," *Brockton Daily Enterprise.*
25. "Messages of Aid, Sympathy, Pouring in to Mayor, Chief," *Brockton Daily Enterprise.*
26. "Disaster Relief Group Organizes," *Brockton Daily Enterprise.*
27. Peck, Strand scrapbook, 53.
28. Ibid., 87.
29. Ibid., 44.
30. "Brockton Fire Fatal to 12 Believed Set," *Daily Boston Globe.*
31. Peck, Strand scrapbook, 104.

Chapter 4

32. LaLiberte, "Strand Disaster," 2.
33. "Injured," *Brockton Daily Enterprise.*
34. Peck, Strand scrapbook, 21.
35. Ibid., 23.
36. "Rugged Firemen Still on Duty, Suffering Injuries," *Brockton Daily Enterprise*; "Sad Scenes at Funeral Parlors, Bereaved Homes," ibid.
37. Peck, Strand scrapbook, 53.
38. William Lipper, e-mail message to Nicole Casper, July 20, 2016.
39. "Another Brockton Theatre Fireman Is Near Death," *Daily Boston Globe.*
40. Remembrance of Daniel C. O'Brien by Robert H. Moore Jr., grandson.
41. Recollection by Frederick Kelley about his father, August 2016.
42. Peck, Strand scrapbook, 62.

Chapter 5

43. "Disaster Relief Group Organizes," *Brockton Daily Enterprise.*
44. Peck, Strand scrapbook, 44.
45. Ibid., 89.
46. "Firemen's Fund Reaches $77,520," *Brockton Daily Enterprise.*
47. "Relief Association in Prompt Payments to Firemen's Widows," *Brockton Daily Enterprise.*
48. "Votes 6–5 for 7½ Restoration," *Brockton Daily Enterprise.*
49. "$28,000 in Relief Fund," *Brockton Daily Enterprise.*
50. "Relief Workers Overwhelmed by Response to Aid Fund," *Brockton Daily Enterprise.*
51. "Tribute to Firemen on Church Calendar," *Brockton Daily Enterprise.*
52. Peck, Strand scrapbook, 101.
53. Ibid., 102.
54. "Unveil Tablet for Strand Fire Dead," *Brockton Daily Enterprise.*
55. "Brockton Remembers Its Heroes," *Enterprise.*
56. Valencia, "Statue Rises in Honor."
57. Kenneth F. Galligan, retired Brockton fire chief, in discussion with Nicole Casper, July 2016.

Epilogue

58. "To Tear Down Perilous Fire Shell," *Brockton Daily Enterprise.*
59. "Brockton Has $150,000 Fire in Shoe Block," *Daily Boston Globe.*
60. Boyle, "Firefighting Has Come Long Way."
61. Galligan, "History of the Brockton Fire Department."
62. Boyle, "Firefighting Has Come Long Way."

Bibliography

Bauman, Stanley A. "Even Cameraman Touched by Sight." *Brockton Daily Enterprise*, March 10, 1941, 9.

Boyle, Maureen. "Firefighting Has Come Long Way Since Strand Tragedy." *Enterprise*, May 8, 2008, A1.

Brockton Daily Enterprise. "Aid Fund Over $15,000." March 13, 1941, 1.

———. "'Bart' Herlihy, 13th Fire Victim Is Laid at Rest" March 15, 1941, 1.

———. "Bells Toll, Firemen Salute as Funeral of McKeraghan Passes Fire Station." March 14, 1941, 1.

———. "City Looks Back on Strand Theatre Horror." March 10, 1942, Second Section.

———. "Clings to Roof When Rafter Falls." March 10, 1941, 8.

———. "Disaster Relief Group Organizes." March 11, 1941, 9.

———. "Doctors, Nurses Rise to Occasion" March 10, 1941, 8.

———. "Eyewitness Accounts Are Given by Sad Firemen." March 10, 1941, 20.

———. "Fire Chief's Club Honors Brockton's Dead Firemen." March 18, 1941, 1.

———. "Fire Destroys Interior of the Empire Theatre." April 7, 1915, 1.

———. "Fireman Herlihy Dies; Is the 13th Victim of Fire" March 13, 1941, 1.

———. "$5,000 in Fund; More Pours In." March 12, 1941, 1.

———. "Fund Committee Goes into Action." March 11, 1941, 1.

———. "Fund Total $53,700; Nashua Remembers." March 22, 1941, 1.

———. "Funerals of 12 Firemen Are Held; Only One Left. March 1, 1941, 2

———. "Individual Funerals for Brockton's Firemen Dead." March 11, 1941, 1.
———. "Injured." March 10, 1941, 8.
———. "'I Should Be There with My Men,' Sobs Deputy Lynch." March 10, 1941, 10.
———. "Like a Routine Fire." March 10, 1941, 1.
———. "Messages of Aid, Sympathy, Pouring in to Mayor, Chief." March 11, 1941, 9.
———. "Nearly $25,000 in Fund." March 14, 1941, 1.
———. "The New Strand Very Handsome," March 2, 1916.
———. "Relief Association in Prompt Payments to Firemen's Widows." March 13, 1941, 10.
———. "Relief Workers Overwhelmed by Response to Aid Fund." March 13, 1941, 10.
———. "Rugged Firemen Still on Duty, Suffering Injuries." March 14, 1941, 10
———. "Sad Scenes at Funeral Parlors, Bereaved Homes." March 11, 1941, 6.
———. "Sick Fireman Hurt 73rd Time." March 11, 1941, 8.
———. "Strand Open, Invite Public." November 29, 1937.
———. "Strand Theatre a Great House." March, 7, 1916.
———. "Stricken Wives Brave in Sorrow." March 10, 1941, 10.
———. "Tells Enterprise Firebug at Work." March 11, 1941, 1.
———. "10 Funerals Make Sad Processions." March 12, 1941, 1.
———. "13 Firemen Lost Lives in Strand, Many More Injured." March 10, 1943, Second Section.
———. "To Tear Down Perilous Fire Shell." April 7, 1941, 1.
———. "Tribute to Firemen on Church Calendar." March 17, 1941, 17.
———. "$28,000 in Relief Fund." March 15, 1941, 1.
———. "Unveil Tablet for Strand Fire Dead" March 11, 1942, Second Section.
———. "Volunteer to Aid Rescuers." March 10, 1941, 12.
———. "Votes 6–5 for 7½ Restoration." March 25, 1941, 1.
———. "Wakes of 12 Firemen Crowded by Mourners." March 12, 1941, 10.
Brockton Firefighters: Concert and Ball Book, 1935. http://www.brockton.ma.us/docs/fire/1935-ball-book.pdf?sfvrsn=2.
Brockton Firefighters: Concert and Ball, 1953. http://www.brockton.ma.us/docs/fire/1953-ball-book.pdf?sfvrsn=2.
"Brockton Firefighters Local 144 Present The 75th Strand Theatre Fire Remembrance." Event program, March 10, 2016. Brockton Fire Museum, Brockton, MA.

"Brockton Firefighters Strand Theatre Memorial Unveiling & Dedication Ceremony." Event program, May 10, 2008. Brockton Fire Museum, Brockton, MA.

Bylaws of the Brockton Firemen's Relief Association, 1956. Brockton Fire Museum, Brockton, MA.

Daily Boston Globe. "Another Brockton Theatre Fireman Is Near Death." March 22, 1941, 3. *ProQuest.* Web. September 4, 2016.

———. "Brockton Fire." April 6, 1941, 2. *ProQuest.* Web. September 4, 2016.

———. "Brockton Fire Fatal to 12 Believed Set." Special Dispatch to, the G. March 12, 1941, 1. *ProQuest.* Web. September 4, 2016.

———. "Brockton Has $150,000 Fire in Shoe Block." December 31, 1942, 1. *ProQuest.* Web. September 4, 2016.

———. "Brockton Pays Last Tribute to 2 Victims." March 14, 1941, 36. *ProQuest.* Web. September 4, 2016.

———. "Fire Nominees at Brockton Quickly Passed." Special Dispatch to, the G. March 18, 1941, 2. *ProQuest.* Web. September 4, 2016.

———. "Herlihy's Death 13th from Brockton Fire." March 13, 1941, 7. *ProQuest.* Web. September 4, 2016.

———. "Memorial Mass Next Tuesday for Brockton Theatre Fire Victims." Special Dispatch to, the G. April 4, 1941, 21. *ProQuest.* Web. September 4, 2016.

———. "Relief Fund Drive for Fire Victims Already Under Way." November 16, 1942, 13. *ProQuest.* Web. September 4, 2016.

———. "Roof Falls, 18 Firemen Buried." Special Dispatch to, the G. March 10, 1941, 1. *ProQuest.* Web. September 4, 2016.

———. "Separate Funerals for Brockton Victims." Special Dispatch to, the G. March 11, 1941, 10. *ProQuest.* Web. September 4, 2016.

Desk Journal Station Six, Brockton Fire Department. July 1, 1940–April 26, 1941. Brockton Fire Museum, Brockton, MA.

Enterprise. "Brockton Remembers Its Heroes." March 11, 2002, A4.

Galligan, Kevin. "A History of the Brockton Fire Department: 150 Years of Service 1846–1996." 1996. http://www.brockton.ma.us/docs/default-source/fire/brockton-fire-department-150th-anniversary.pdf?sfvrsn=2.

LaLiberte, E. Joseph. "The Strand Disaster." Unpublished eyewitness account. Courtesy of the E. Joseph LaLiberte Estate.

Lyons, Cornelius, F. "Enterprise Man Aids in Rescue." *Brockton Daily Enterprise*, March 10, 1941, 1.

Peck, Phyllis E. Strand scrapbook. 1941. Brockton Fire Museum, Brockton, MA.

Pitcher, Mark, "Remembering the Strand Theatre, Brockton Fire Department History, ND." http://www.brockton.ma.us/docs/fire/remembering-the-strand-theater.pdf?sfvrsn=4.

Valencia, Milton, J. "A Statue Rises in Honor of Brockton Firefighters Killed in '41." *Boston Globe*, May 11, 2008, B.3

Willard, Donald. "F.D.R. to Ask 3 Billion for Aid: Blame Flimsy Roof for Brockton Theatre Fire Deaths French Navy Set to Convoy Food 12 Firemen Dead, 9 in Hospital in Theatre Fire; Brockton Rallies to Kin; 25 Children Fatherless." *Daily Boston Globe*, March 11 1941, 1. *ProQuest.* Web. September 4, 2016.

Wilmeth, Don B., and Tice L. Miller. *The Cambridge Guide to American Theatre.* Cambridge, UK: Cambridge University Press, 1993.

Index

About the Authors

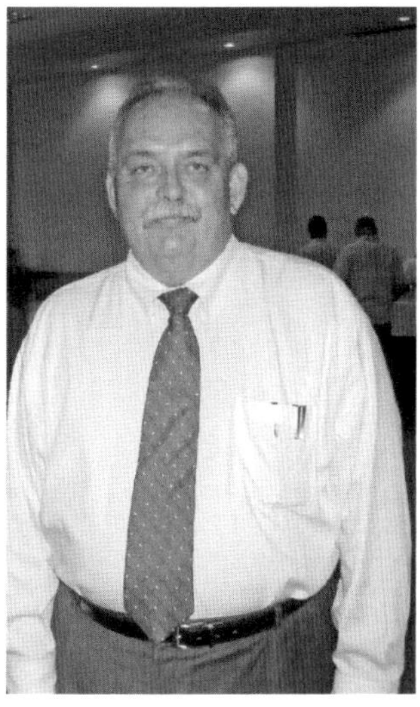

Coauthor James E. Benson is the past president of the Brockton Historical Society and Fire Museum and serves as the organization's official city historian. Benson has a BA in history from Muhlenberg College and is currently the parish administrator at Brockton's historic First Lutheran Church. A resident of West Bridgewater, he serves as chairman of that town's historical commission and is an active member of several civic organizations locally and regionally. Benson coauthored *The Swedes of Greater Brockton* in Arcadia Publishing's Images of America series and has authored *West Bridgewater*, *Brockton* and *Brockton Revisited* in the same series, as well as *Along Old Canada Road* and *Brockton* in the Postcard History series published by Arcadia Publishing.

Coauthor Nicole B. Casper has worked as the director of Archives and Special Collections and has been assistant professor at Stonehill College since 2001. She received her BA in history from Stonehill College and MLS from Simmons College. She also serves on the board of the trustees at the Brockton Historical Society. She is the author of the Stonehill publications

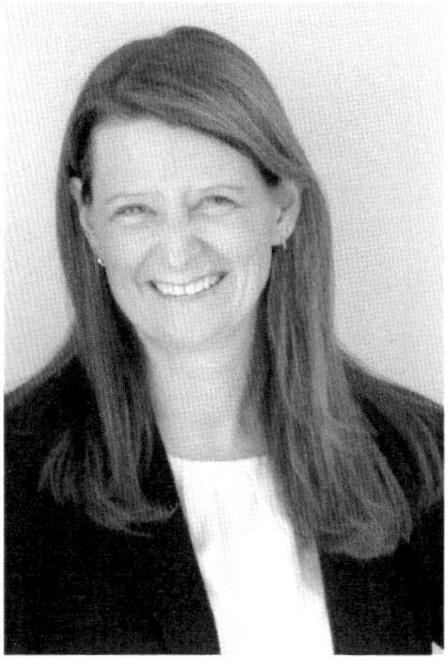

"A Historical Profile of Stonehill College" and "A Look Back: Celebrating the Centennial of Donahue and Alumni Halls." A native of Rhode Island, she currently lives in Attleboro, Massachusetts, with her husband. In addition to her love of history, she enjoys quilting and combined the two in 2008 with the completion of a photo quilt titled the Brockton "Shoe" Fly quilt, featuring historical images of the Brockton Shoe Industry, which was part of the exhibit *The Perfect Fit*, organized by the Fuller Craft Museum, Brockton, Massachusetts.